# Character Is King

## God's Destination for You

**John Binkley**

Guy Thing Press
Southlake, TX

Character Is King: God's Destination for You, by John Binkley
Published by Guy Thing Press
P.O. Box 827
Roanoke, TX 76242

Guy Thing Press books may be purchased in bulk for educational, business, fund-raising, or sales promotional use. For more information, please contact Guy Thing Press.

Please visit us at www.guythingpress.com

Unless otherwise noted, all Scripture quotations are from the *New King James Version of the Bible,* Copyright 1979, 1980, 1982, 1984, Thomas Nelson Inc.

*Printed in the United States of America*

ISBN-13: 978-0-9786291-2-0
ISBN-10: 0-9786291-2-4

This book is dedicated to our son Hal Binkley, John Harold Binkley III. A man who epitomizes the faithfulness of God. A man whose love, encouragement and obedient faith has been the catalyst for so much of my life.

It has been said that heroes are those who, in a moment of time, act on a need greater than themselves. For that reason and many more Hal is...and always will be..."my hero."

# ACKNOWLEDGEMENTS

This book is comprised of lessons I have learned in my life. These lessons are not theory; they are facts that I have proven in my life and continue to prove day by day. Wisdom comes through personal experience and from the teachings and examples of others. The wisdom in this book was gathered from many men whom I respect greatly. Few of the ideas of this book were created by me; they were borrowed from others; but I have lived and proven all of the ideas. I am deeply grateful to the men who have been my role models and who have mentored me, both personally and through their books and tapes.

It is my prayer that as you apply these principles to your life, that you will have the abundant and fulfilling life that our Father in heaven has ordained for you.

# CONTENTS

# FOREWORD

In the Book of James, Elijah is described as a man with a nature like ours, indeed all who have come before us are men and women with a nature likes ours. This book clearly outlines the process to rise above our human nature and assume the posture of divine purpose and destiny.

The "dominion commission" as presented in scripture and outlined in this book is the destiny of the ecclesia, the victory of mankind and the triumph of God. From Genesis to Revelation this destiny and commission is restated as God's will and purpose for those called by His name.

Dr. John Binkley has a clear vision of the purpose, power and potential of this great commission. Like the Hebrew prophet Elisha who succeeded the prophet Elijah when his time on earth was finished, Dr. John Harold Binkley, Jr. continues the legacy of his teacher and mentor, the late Dr. Edwin Louis Cole.

In that respect, Dr. Binkley is a true 21st Century Elisha. In addition to having become an excellent author, he is lecturing, teaching and mentoring men world wide.

This book is being used as curriculum to teach the "dominion commission" by Phoenix University of Theology. It brings the commission and destiny of the faithful to a level of practical application and implementation.

Dr. Richard Drake, president
Phoenix University of Theology

# INTRODUCTION

Several hundred years ago, when European pioneers were exploring and settling this continent, many areas of the country were unknown to them. As these adventurers and explorers wandered back into the settlements, local mapmakers interviewed them, repeatedly asking, "What is out there?" and probing for new information. These adventurers were men that were willing to go beyond the map to explore the unknown. That sense of adventure lives on today in those who are willing to go beyond the map in our personal lives or in business. When we go beyond the map, we go places that we have never been before, see things we have never seen before, and think thoughts that we have never thought before—all so that we will become what we have never been before.

God wants to take each of us beyond the map to a place He calls Destiny. The Bible often speaks of that, particularly in Ephesians where it states that we are His workmanship, created in Christ Jesus unto good works, in which God has ordained that we should walk. [1] We have been ordained since the beginning of time and predestined for a specific purpose. I believe that our purpose, our destiny, is surrounded by the gifting God has given us. The essence of the kingdom is to discover our gifts and develop them, to use them, and to operate for God's glory.

God had a destiny for Israel called the Promised Land. Although God brought them to its border and intended to give them the land, they stubbornly refused to go forward because of fears of possible problems with the giants that inhabited the land. We are like Israel in many ways in that we get comfortable where we are and hold back; then we begin to see things to fear. Studies show that we have a tendency to grow to the level of our comfort zone, which is where most people end up living. No special effort, no diligence and no discipline are required in the comfort zone because nothing is happening there. When we are comfortable, we already know what to expect. If we are not progressing, however, we are regressing because there is no such place as a static, stagnant, standstill relationship. God wants us to be constantly moving toward the destiny He has planned for us.

That is what He wanted for Israel too, but they chose to wander around in the wilderness for forty years, where they were comfortable. They came out of bondage in Egypt, where they had lived in the land of "not enough," and found themselves in the wilderness, the land of "just enough"; but God wanted to take them to the Promised Land, the land of "more than enough." That is where God wants to take each of us as well. It is part of our destiny, and He has a plan for getting us there.

As Dr. Edwin Louis Cole, founder of the Christian Men's Network, has taught, God does everything according to a pattern and based upon the principles of His kingdom. In His kingdom, as in athletic competitions, we will not win unless we compete "lawfully, fairly, according to the rules laid down." [2] This book is about doing things God's way, the kingdom way. [3] That is why in this book we will find the biblical pattern for fulfilling God's ordained destiny in our lives, the pattern in which to reach our destination.

I hope that you will enjoy this journey beyond the map and discover the joys, adventures and fulfillment that, in your secret heart, you have always known belonged to you. Reach out and take them for they are yours. They are your destiny.

# • CHAPTER ONE •

## POWER OF A DREAM

Dreams are the basis of every great achievement, the foundation of every great accomplishment. Dreams reflect our soul and reveal what is in our heart. If our dreams are real enough, they will be stronger than our fears. If our dreams are strong enough, they will overcome our lack of discipline and small thinking. If our dreams are powerful enough, they will lead us to heights we can only imagine. Dreams are the secret power that overcomes every adversity, obstacle or impediment that stands between victory and us. I know this to be true because I have applied the principles in this book to my own life and have achieved both influence and affluence. My dreams, directed by these principles, have allowed me the financial freedom to travel to fifty-three countries. I have found the following seven propositions about dreams to be life changing.

## Proposition 1. Dream big dreams

A dream is a vision, a pictured goal that gives direction to a destination, a road map to our destiny. The Bible says that without a vision, we will perish.[4] Without the dream, we will not know where we are going or when we arrive. A dream is different from a fantasy, which is birthed in unreality and focuses on oneself; a fantasy leads to a possible and temporary success. A dream is birthed in reality and always serves others; it leads to a certain and permanent significance. A fantasy is temporal and selfish, while a dream is eternal and selfless.

3

A dream pushes us out of our comfort zone. Nothing exciting or new ever happens in the comfort zone, mainly because we do not *do* anything there. We tend to settle down into our ruts and go robot-like through each day with the same routines, the same thoughts, the same actions. It is so easy for us to become comfortable; in the meantime everything around us falls into shambles while we sit: the weeds grow in the lawn, the repairs around the house go unmade, self-help courses lay unfinished, the children are untrained and undisciplined, friendships deteriorate from lack of care, projects lay untouched. We drown in our own comfort and have not the energy to pull ourselves out. There is, however, a way out; in chapter eight we will discuss in detail what we can do to survive the comfort zone.

For now, though, consider Gideon, a judge of ancient Israel, whose dream thrust him out of the comfort zone into real action that saved his nation. We know Gideon was a wimp. According to his own testimony, he had never accomplished anything significant or noteworthy in his life. For seven years, roving bands of robbers had overrun his country—nothing seemed to stop them. They took what they wanted, when they wanted and wreaked terrible devastation, leaving the people in abject poverty. Only what could be concealed in mountainous caves, wine presses and such places escaped their plunder.

Gideon was in a wine press sifting wheat and grain, hiding from his enemies, when an angel of the Lord came to him and said, "Gideon, you mighty man of valor." I believe that Gideon had a dream. I believe that he knew in his heart that God had something significantly better for him than where he was at that particular point in his life. He had never done anything valiant, noteworthy, or significant, but he wanted to. He had never done anything courageous, he was not what he wanted to be, but he still wanted to be. Gideon was not what he wanted to be; he wanted to be more. He had a dream, but he had never acted upon it. Maybe that is why Gideon was focusing only on surviving.

A dream reveals the level of our life—survivor, success, or significance. Gideon was definitely at the lowest level; he was struggling to survive yet the angel addressed him as though he was of significance, "Gideon, you mighty man of valor, the Lord is with you!"

Gideon was like you and me: He was not what he wanted to be. He had not done anything significant or noteworthy in his life, but wanted to. When God said, "Gideon, you mighty man of valor," He was speaking to the dream God had placed in his heart. Gideon went from a zero to a hero in an instant. I have been in those circumstances. Usually when God speaks to you about your dream, your destiny, you are in contradictory circumstances. Gideon was in contradictory circumstances. He and the other children of God were hiding in dens and caves; they were hiding from their enemies, those roving Midianites who were ravaging the land like a plague of locusts. For God to call Gideon a mighty man of valor when he is hiding in a pit, a hole in the ground, these are contradictory circumstances.

In an instant, Gideon moved from the level of survival to the level of significance. After his initial obedience, the Spirit of the Lord came upon Gideon and led him to completely destroy the marauders and deliver Israel from the hand of their enemies. This was not an easy task but Gideon's dream was never about himself; it was always about the deliverance of his people and his country. His dream was sorely tested before God gave him that life of significance. Later in this chapter, we will return to Gideon to look at how he overcame those tests. For now, it is important that we know that our dream will never be only about ourselves. In order for it to endure and provide the impetus for us to overcome obstacles, it must be based on the needs of others.

Gideon moved from the level of focusing on himself and struggling to survive to a life of significance, of focusing on others. We all live on one of these three levels: survivor, success, or significance. Most people live as survivors. Day in and day out, year in and year out—barely getting by. Just surviving. About twenty-five percent of us live on a level of success. Success, however, is only temporary and is focused on ourselves. Our lives are significant by our service to others, and therein lies greatness. Just as there is a difference between being famous and being great, so there is a difference between being successful and being significant. Madonna is famous and successful. Mother Teresa was great; her life was significant because it focused on others. Jesus told us that our care of others is the measure of our greatness.

Like Gideon, I was living on the survivor level when I discovered the principles in this book. I had lost my job and was struggling. I had been a Christian for three or four years and was searching for a message from God when I heard Dr. Edwin Louis Cole say, "Champions are not those who never fail; champions are those who never quit." He went on to emphasize, "You're never too old, you're never too young, and it's never too late to fulfill your God-ordained destiny." I took that word from Dr. Cole and, although he had never met me, he mentored me through his books and tapes. I learned that the Bible gives us principles to live by, promises to believe in, examples to follow, and commandments to obey. I learned also that God does everything according to a pattern based on a principle of His kingdom. When we base our lives on the principles of His kingdom, we have the key that will reveal God's plan for our lives. "I know the thoughts that I have for you, says the Lord. They are plans for good and not for evil, to give you a future and a hope. In those days when you pray, I will listen. You will find me when you seek me, if you look for me in earnest." [5]

## Proposition 2. We are not created equal

We were created special, not equally gifted. In Paul's famous analogy of the Body of Christ, he refers to the various parts of the body having different functions, needs, and abilities. [6] Again, in the story of the talents, the master leaves talents with his servants to invest while he is out of the country; he proportions the talents according to each one's ability to handle that amount. [7] Similarly, our gifts, abilities, and talents determine our destiny.

It is easy to see that we do not have the same gifts; if so, we would all be mathematicians, or physicists, or salespersons. If we all had the same physical gifts, there would never be a winner of a foot race because we would all finish in a tie. If we had the same artistic gifts, we would be equally good in sketching, music, and singing. Instead, no one is just like another; no two exactly look alike, walk alike, talk alike, or think alike. No two fingerprints are the same; no two voice prints are the same; no two iris prints are the same. Each of us is a unique Designer original! He has never run out of designs; each child is endowed with his own identity—completely and uniquely his—and with gifts that determine his destiny.

Our gifts and strengths, not our weaknesses, make for excellence. The problem is that we generally focus more on the weaknesses because we are negative by nature. In a simple test of listing strengths and weaknesses, most people will list fifteen to twenty weaknesses to every five strengths. We have been taught erroneously that by focusing on the weaknesses we will improve and become excellent in every area. That simply is not true. We may improve the weaknesses to average, but we neglect the strengths

6

that could have made us excellent. We should focus, instead, on the special endowment that God placed within to enable us to do superior things. When we discover the one thing that we can do better than almost anybody else does, that is God's pattern for our lives.

## Proposition 3. Character is the key—your talent can take you where your character cannot sustain you.

Character is our most important attribute. God and men commit to character, not to talent. Unfortunately, many employers and women are overly impressed by talent and fail to see the underlying character of the person. Therefore, a highly talented individual is hired and the employer soon discovers that the person's character cannot support the talent, and this leads to conflict and an eventual firing. Or, a woman falls in love with a highly talented person and discovers he is a self-centered jerk; his character is so flawed that it leads to a painful and abortive relationship. This is not to imply that all highly talented people have no character; far from it, many successful people have strong character undergirding their talents.

This undergirding is first visible in the form of faithfulness, which is the foundation of character. Faithfulness is determined by how we handle the small details in a project, by how we handle our own or another's money, and by how we handle our relationships. Details, money, relationships: how we handle these vital issues reveals either the strength or lack of character. Our talent can take us where our character cannot sustain us. Since we will discuss the various aspects of character in depth in chapter two, it is appropriate to move on to seedtime and harvest.

## Proposition 4. Embrace the principle of seedtime and harvest

Delayed gratification teaches principles of increase. In the story of the talents, the master gave out various amounts to his servants and after a *long time* he returned to receive his interest. "Long time" speaks of seedtime and harvest: a time of preparing the soil, planting, watering, de-weeding, and finally harvest. The principle here is that God will give us all the time we need to develop our talent, and just because it may take a long time before we see an increase on our investment does not mean that the increase is not coming. Sadly, in our instant society few of us know how to postpone gratification until everything is perfect and the timing is right. Our grandparents or great-grandparents probably grasped the concept of waiting better. They understood that sowing and reaping follow definite rules and that time is the basic ingredient. It takes time to grow the perfect October apple, to grow a towering oak, to write an excellent book, to hand-carve a *Moses* or *La Pieta*, to paint a *Mona Lisa*, to build a watch, to rear a child. Similarly, it takes time to perfect a skill, to build a sound financial portfolio, to develop a muscle, to become a man or woman of God. Time is the fabric of our days, yet we have so little of it. Embracing the principle of seedtime and harvest means being willing to wait for our dream to germinate, develop and grow to full maturity before we seek self-gratification; it is understanding that during the wait tests and challenges, like weeds and pests, will surface.

## Proposition 5. Overcome our fears

Our dream will be tested just as Gideon's dream was tested. He probably dreamed of being a man of courage and discipline but he lived in a fear-filled country where marauders outnumbered and overran the citizens and left behind misery and heartbreak. He lived without hope of ever being delivered from the hands of his enemy. He was tormented and afflicted, but in the mist of that hopelessness, he had a dream.

Dreams always seem to come in contradictory circumstances. Solomon wrote in Ecclesiastes that if we wait for all the conditions to be right, we will never get anything done. [8] I can imagine that Gideon was considered a loser, a wimp, a nobody by his community. He admitted to being the least of the smallest tribe. From casual observance, there was nothing noteworthy, significant or valiant about Gideon. Yet the angel spoke of his destiny and the dream in his heart. A dream always speaks of destiny, not history nor the present. It did not matter to the angel that Gideon had no history as a warrior, that he had no prospects for the future; all that mattered was the dream of deliverance and freedom that burned in Gideon's heart.

Several years ago, St. Paul Insurance Company ran a television commercial that showed a rhinoceros racing across the plain toward a slight young girl of about ten years. There is no voice, only the blood-charging music that accompanies the thundering hooves of this two-ton creature approaching the girl with the speed of a horse. Across the screen rolls the words, "Trust is not being afraid, even when you are vulnerable."

Gideon was certainly vulnerable; the odds against him were overwhelming but he must have been encouraged when God promised to be with him. He even called Gideon "mighty man of valor." Valor derives from the Hebrew *chayil*, which means "strong, virtuous, wealthy, forceful, powerful." This is how God saw Gideon, and I believe that is how God sees us. If defeat is not a possibility, then victory means nothing. It is also said that when a dream does not appear possible, that is where God is. In obedience, Gideon sounded the trumpet summoning the troops to battle. Then God pulled a surprise on him, teaching him the ultimate in discipline.

## Proposition 6. Embrace discipline

Gideon went from a zero to a hero almost immediately. Thirty-two thousand troops responded and joined him on the mountainside above the enemy—32,000 against 135,000! Then God said, "There are too many of you."

"Too many? One against more than four is too many?"

"Yes, send the fearful ones home." Twenty-two thousand left immediately.

"There are still too many. Give them the water test, and send home those who focus on their own needs." Nine thousand and seven hundred went home.

Three hundred remained. At this point, Gideon understood that he had to want his dream more than he wanted anything else. Gideon and God had several heart-to-heart conversations, with Gideon trying to discover whether his dream was really from God or simply ambition.

"If this is really you, God, let this fleece be wet in the morning and the ground be dry." The next morning he wrung out enough water to fill a bowl. "Okay, God, let's try a different tactic, if this dream is from you, let the fleece be dry and the ground be wet." He picked up a dry fleece the next morning. The reduction of his troops apparently led to the most serious conversations and caused God to send Gideon on a reconnaissance mission. As he crept up to one of the enemy's tents, he overheard a man relating a dream that had just awakened him, a strange dream of a huge loaf of barley bread tumbling into the camp and knocking the tents flat.

"Your dream can mean only one thing! Gideon, the son of Joash, the Israeli, is going to come and massacre all the allied forces of Midian," the companion of the dreamer exclaimed. [9]

Gideon thanked God and then raced up the mountainside, roused his troops and armed them with the only weapons he had: trumpets, clay pots, torches, and a battle cry, "For the Lord and for Gideon!" Just after midnight, Gideon and his troops silently surrounded the perimeter of the enemy's camp. As the guard was changing, the Israelis blew their trumpets, broke the pots, waved the torches and cried, "For the Lord and for Gideon!" God caused confusion to settle over the camp and Gideon's Three Hundred stood and watched while the enemy slaughtered each other. This victory came because Gideon disciplined himself to follow God's instructions meticulously.

Discipline, or self-government, is the essence of the kingdom. First, it is necessary that we allow the Word of God to correct, mold, and perfect our mental faculties and character; because there is no direction to a destination without correction. Second, we must then submit to following God's plan, doing things God's way and in God's timing. Without such discipline, we are subject to empire-building, aberrant morality, and certain defeat.

## Proposition 7. Embrace failure

Champions are not those who never fail, champions are those who never quit. Many of us hide our dreams and talents because we are afraid of failure. This fear is probably the greatest obstacle to fulfilling our destinies. In the story of the talents, the man who hid his talent was not condemned for failing, but rather for hiding the talent and refusing to use it. If he had tried and failed, God would not have condemned him for failing; He condemned him for not trying. I have tried many things in my life and I have failed at many of them, but I have learned a valuable lesson…NEVER QUIT! Failure is not the worst thing that can happen to us; quitting is. Besides, we have not failed until we quit. In chapter nine, I will show you how to fail your way to success.

## Every dream will be tested

How do we know whether our dream is from God and not from ambition? How do we know the dream is real? It is actually fairly easy: ambition serves the self, the ego; a dream from God serves Christ first and then others. Each dream, however, will be tested in two ways.

**Test 1. By fear.** Both faith and fear attract. Faith attracts the positive; fear attracts the negative. Faith and fear are much alike, in that both embrace and believe in something that has not yet happened. Among Gideon's troops, two out of three were afraid and went home. Consider this, they probably knew about the angel's visit to Gideon and about God's promise to deliver the country from the marauders, but they took one look at the overwhelming numbers of the opposing side and became afraid. I believe God had Gideon send them home because He knew their fear would contaminate the other troops and jeopardize the battle. Fear is the greatest impediment to fulfilling our destiny. Most of us are afraid of many things but we hide it under bravado. We have fears concerning the quality of our work, about the progress of our careers. In a social context, we fear intimacy, being vulnerable, making commitments, being transparent with women. Though we would never admit it, we men fear war and death. Rarely do we let our true feelings show, even when we are close to God. We are afraid He will find out who we really are, as if He doesn't *already* know!

Our destiny, what we are called to be, causes us a lot of fear, too. Usually presenting with symptoms of great anxiety, timidity and loss of courage, fear is always present. God, however, does not give us a spirit of fear; instead, He gives love, power, and a sound mind. [10] Fear comes because Satan tries to sabotage our relationship with God, but fear cannot paralyze us or stop us if our dream is real, if it is from God. A good rule of thumb is to check the source of a dream. If we can fulfill our dream in our natural ability, God did not call us to it. If the dream seems beyond our abilities, that is when we need total dependence on God and when Satan tries to instill fear.

Fear is always the first test. Are we afraid? So have thousands before us been afraid. Without a dream or a vision we will not be courageous, we will run. If fear is the primary test, what is the answer to fear? The antidote to fear is a bigger dream. If our dream is bigger than our fear, it will overcome our fear. It will not destroy our fear, because fear will always be present; but it will overcome the fear. Having a powerful dream is what causes men to come from adverse circumstances and achieve great things. Having a powerful dream is what causes people to continue pushing, sometimes to their dying day, to achieve their purposes. Having a powerful dream is what causes patriots to birth a free democracy, and single mothers to put children through college, and fathers to sacrifice themselves for the advancement of their children. It is never easy to fulfill a dream; it requires tremendous vision and trust in God.

Only our dream will cause us to persist and persevere. Persistence comes from knowing in our heart that our dream is worth pursuing, against all odds. Persistence will always overcome resistance. The difference between men who succeed and men who fail is in their ability to handle pressure. If we cannot stand the pressure of adversity, we are indeed poor specimens of manhood. Others will always resist our dream, and their very resistance becomes a form of testing. We will notice that after 22,000 of his troops returned home because they were afraid, Gideon did not quit. He persisted even when he had to send home 9,700 more because they were not focused on the outcome. He persisted with only three hundred men, against 135,000 highly trained warriors. Gideon persisted toward the fulfillment of his dream because he was disciplined, which is the second test.

**Test 2. Through discipline.** Every dream is tested through the presence or lack of discipline. When the chips were down, Gideon chose the men whose view of the dream was larger than their thirst. Their focus was more on the upcoming battle than on their personal need for water. The essence of the kingdom is discipline. The more self-government we have, the less external government we will need. We all know what to do; we understand that dreams take time to fulfill and that we need to allow for seedtime and harvest. We know to be faithful in small things if we expect to be given responsibility in larger things. We know to be good stewards of our money, that if we are not we cannot expect more. We know to be faithful in handling another man's things. We know that maturity means growing up and thinking like an adult, it means putting childish things behind us. No matter what we accomplish in life, we cannot achieve it without discipline. Why can we not lose weight? Exercise? Control our temper? Study the success strategies of others? Control our passion? Study the Bible? Hear from God? No discipline. Without discipline, we have no dream, no vision and no hope of anything better.

## Dreams propel us toward promotions

Promotions come when we are driven by the dream to embrace discipline, develop character and overcome all obstacles. First, we closely follow God's plan, purpose, and destiny, and concentrate on overcoming all obstacles, refusing to see anything larger than our dream. This is particularly important in overcoming such obstacles as persecution, racism, failure, poverty, and social stigmas. Second, we focus on building our character by becoming a better person and by practicing stewardship in all things: talents, gifts, anointing, time for our children and wife and God's Word. Third, we embrace discipline and train ourselves, carefully study our industry, and conscientiously develop a business plan to facilitate achieving the dream.

Character, not talent or looks or personality, is the deciding factor in any promotion. That is because God commits to character, not talent, and so do men of wisdom. Wise men commit to character; they are more interested in *who* we are than in *what* we can do. When the angel of the Lord saluted Gideon, he called him a "mighty man of valor." [11] The word used here for man is the Hebrew *gibbowr* or *gibbor* (both forms are pronounced ghib-bore´), which means "powerful; by implication, warrior, tyrant." In the King James Version, it is rendered "champion, chief." In the Septuagint or Greek Version of the Old Testament, it is translated as "excel, giant, man, mighty (man, one), strong (man), valiant man." By calling him a man of valor, the Angel of the Lord was calling Gideon a champion, a strong man. Valor implies having "strength of mind or spirit that enables a man to encounter danger with firmness; personal bravery." [12] Essentially, valor means "courage." Developing good character makes us men and women of valor. With character, we have the strength to stand firm on our beliefs. With character, we will not compromise either God's principles or His Word. With character, we choose not to wallow in sin and mediocrity. With character, everything we do aligns with God's Word and we strive for excellence. Character, however, like a physical muscle, is developed through progressive resistance, tests and discipline. A quick look at Israel's journey to her destiny will make this more understandable.

## Summary

- We must go beyond the map to seek new horizons. We must go where we have never been before, to become what we have never been before.

- Unless we attempt to do something beyond what we have already mastered, we will never grow.

- God has a destiny for us, a destination where He wants to take us.

- A genuine, authentic dream will overcome and vanquish every fear.

- We live our lives on three levels: survivor, successful, or significant.

- Significant people live their lives for the benefit of others.

- The Bible gives us promises to believe in, principles to live by, examples to follow and commandments to obey.

- Everything God does, He does according to a pattern, and based on a principle of His kingdom.

- We are not created equal to others; we are created special.

- God created us unique and special, for us to operate in excellence.

- Character development is more important than talent development. God commits to character, not to talent.

- Time is required for anything to grow. This is true in a financial portfolio, true in muscle development, true in the development of talents, and it is true in the development of Christlike character.

- Embrace delayed gratification.

- Every dream will be tested for its authenticity and validity.

- Discipline, or self-government, is the essence of the kingdom.

- There can be no direction from God without correction from God.

- Both faith and fear attract. Faith attracts the positive. Fear attracts the negative. Both faith and fear believe in something that has not yet happened.

- Persistence will always overcome resistance.

- Unless we have a dream or vision of something better for our life, we will never experience it.

- God made us to be champions.

- Christlike character is your destiny.

# • CHAPTER TWO •

## IT IS ALL ABOUT CHARACTER

Although the Israelites had spent four hundred years in Egypt, the land of not enough, slavery was not their destiny. God wanted to take them to the Promised Land, the land of more than enough, but because they rebelled against His plan, they wandered for forty years around the wilderness of just enough. Finally, He brought them to the edge of the Promised Land and instructed them to send twelve spies into the land. Ignoring God's plan, ten of those spies reported, "We cannot take the land because there are giants there"; but two, Caleb and Joshua, declared, "Yes, we can!" Think about it for a moment. What would it have taken for Israel to go into the Promised Land? It would have taken spiritual knowledge and faith, wouldn't it? It would have taken hope, courage, creativity, wisdom, favor, tenacity, perseverance and belief. God wants us to possess these attributes so that we can overcome obstacles and fulfill our destiny.

## Character is the most important issue in determining and fulfilling our destiny

We are created in God's image and in His likeness; therefore, we have the potential to share God's character attributes. Every obstacle standing between our destiny and us is nothing more than a test to measure our spiritual maturity and character. Maturation of character is a process, not an event; it does not happen overnight. It takes years, indeed even

**15**

a lifetime, to build character; but God is a gradualist. He understands that without resistance, strength cannot be developed. He allows each challenge we face and gives us the ability to conquer it or it would not be there. He never allows us to be tested beyond our ability to withstand. God will never allow us to get in a fight that we cannot win. We can overcome anything through the power of the Holy Spirit.

## Our character is based on our knowledge of God

Knowing God comes through proving and testing His character. Therefore we must seek Him first, above our dream, our ambition, our goals. If we would really know God and His ways, it is absolutely vital that we seek *Him*, not what men say about Him. We must learn how He manages His kingdom and how He operates. One of the first things we will learn is that as we seek His kingdom and His righteousness He will add blessings, benefits, and favor to us. [13] Second, we were created for His glory. [14] Third, we were created to declare His praise. [15] Fourth, without faith it is impossible to please Him. Fifth, He rewards those who seek Him diligently. [16] Sixth, we are never out of His thoughts. [17] In fact, He has established a destiny for us that involves increase and abundance. If we are tired of our present situation and level of abundance and desire to fulfill this destiny, we must move up to the next level, which starts with knowing who we are and knowing our relationship with God. Sadly, because of lack of training in spiritual matters many of us fail to see ourselves as having any relationship with God. Yet God says He has created us for His glory. [18]

*In kabode*, the Hebrew word used in Isaiah 43:7 and that is translated "glory" in English, means that we are God's honor. We are God's splendor. We are God's power. We are God's wealth. We are...God's authority... His magnificence... His fame...His dignity...His riches...His excellency. Ephesians 2:10 says we are His workmanship, designed especially by God for a purpose. [19] We were created to do good works, *agothos ergon,* which means we are to be productive and beneficial in the work of our hands. Those things that occupy our hands, our employment or our product, are to be beneficial and excellent. When they are, increase is automatic.

We must believe God has something *significantly* better for us. We were created to increase because we have a mission to fulfill. Everything that God does is based on the principles of His kingdom and is done according to a pattern. Most of the patterns that pertain to our life will be found in the parables of the New Testament or in the stories of the Old Testament. While everyone is familiar with the Great Commission of the New Testament, few are aware that there is also a Great Commission of the Old Testament. It is found in Genesis 1:26 and reads in part, "And God said, Let us make man in our image, after our likeness: and let them have dominion." [20] Then in verse 28, God commissioned man, who had just been created, to rule the earth. "And God blessed them, and God said unto them, Be fruitful, and multiply, and replenish the earth, and subdue it: and have dominion over the fish of the sea, and over the fowl of the air, and over every living thing that moveth upon the earth."

The earth is the Lord's and is, therefore, His people's stewardship. We are in God's family business and are joined with Him in the enterprise of establishing His kingdom on earth as it is in heaven. [21] Earth is where we have authority. God wants the conditions of heaven to be brought to earth and He expects us to be faithful stewards. [22] So as we apply God's kingdom principles to the created order, we bring God's will to cover the earth.

He authorized us to have dominion over everything on the earth. Dominion, *radah,* means to prevail against, to subjugate, and to establish authority and to rule over. Dominion is to establish influence and authority in every area of life. Dominion is influence, and influence is leadership. This dominion is not our own, however; since we are God's glory, we are to establish His authority, His divine majesty, and His sovereignty over the earth. How then is this dominion to be effected? Through fulfilling, individually, our destinies. John wrote, in Revelation 1:6, "And [Jesus Christ] hath made us kings and priests unto God and his Father; to him be glory and dominion for ever and ever. Amen." We are God-ordained to be either a priest or a king, as determined by our gifts and talents.

One of the reasons the earth has not been covered with the glory of God, and God's sovereignty has not been established is that the kings have not been doing their job. They have not understood the job description; have not felt appreciated, vital or necessary to the task of establishing the dominion of the kingdom of God. Instead, the church has focused on ministry and the priesthood of the believer to the point that the common belief has been that committed Christians must have a pulpit ministry. This belief has left the majority of believers stranded, with no hope of fulfilling the Great Commission of the Old Testament. Consequently, many have assumed they have no part in the spread of the kingdom, in the glory of God, in the honor of God, in the power of God; so they have led lives of frustration and resignation, wanting to be a part of the kingdom but knowing they have not the gifts required for public ministry. Is this true? Has God eliminated two-thirds of His children from participating in His kingdom?

No! This deception comes from our unrelenting enemy, Satan, whose goal is to deceive and enslave. Since the beginning, he has been planting doubt concerning God's motives in the minds of mankind, trying to divert us from the destiny God has chosen for us. [23] Satan wars for our minds, primarily using four techniques: (1) he disparages the truth and makes us believe the truth is a lie; [24] (2) he blinds our minds so that we cannot receive the gospel of Jesus Christ; [25] (3) he makes us believe we war against the physical rather than spiritual; [26] and (4) he makes us believe we can do things our way. [27] Doing things our way is deception. We may have righteous and noble intentions, but unless we do things God's way we are deceived.

## Character is developed by doing things God's way

Our defense is to do things God's way. First, we must seek God's presence and His purpose and major in the Word of God. We must learn to think as He thinks. [28] Until we know the Word of God, we will never know what His purpose for us is, we will never know Him, and we will never have faith. In fact, our faith will never rise above our knowledge of God's Word. Therefore, it is important that we meditate on the Word continually and let it renew our minds to God's will and way. Aside from the study of the Word itself, which is absolutely vital, we can renew our minds through tapes, books and videos about the Word and through uplifting spiritual music. Seminars that provide solid Christian teaching are another way to renew our minds. Without knowing His Word, we will never know obedience because we cannot know if we are transgressing. If we are transgressing God's Word, He cannot bless us.

Meditating on God's Word means to turn it over in our minds continually, to reflect on it, to become absorbed with it and repeat it thoughtfully, to imagine it, to envision it and bring it to the mind's eye, to conceive it in thought. In other words, meditating on God's Word is to keep it ever before our minds so that it affects not only our thoughts but also our actions. As we do this, we will know God's ways, His voice, and His presence. This renewing of our minds will transform our character to be like His character and teach us to know God's perfect will. [29]

Meditation puts us in the place to perform God's Word: doing His Will, in His Way, in His Wisdom, and according to His Word. [30] Meditation, however, is not a one-time exercise that will solve all our problems. We must keep meditating until we see ourselves doing that thing for which we are expecting God's help. [31] We must also release all worry; worry is negative meditation that distracts us from focusing on God's Word. Besides, God has promised that those who live in His presence shall be safe[32] and that He will teach them to prosper. [33]

As we meditate on and obey God's Word, we will be given favor with men. [34] God's wisdom will light our way, [35, 36] and He will open doors that no mere man can open. David wrote about what happens to a man who meditates continually upon God's Word: "His delight is in the law of the Lord, and in His law he meditates day and night. And he shall be like a tree planted by the rivers of water, that bringeth forth his fruit in his season; his leaf also shall not wither; and whatsoever he doeth shall prosper." [37] In these verses, he lists five results of meditating on God's Word. First, the man who meditates shall be "like a tree planted," one that has been carefully selected, cultivated and pruned for maximum growth. This man is not a wild, stunted tree overrun with brambles, briers, thorns, and thistles. He has been planted in the proper soil and positioned to receive the necessary water and sunlight to maximize his growth. Second, the man who meditates is "planted by rivers of water." This phrase alludes to an ancient system of irrigation in which sluices were cut from a river to conduct a stream of water into certain portions of a field. These sluices were blocked by large pieces of sod, which were moved aside by the farmer's foot when he wanted to direct the water to a particular crop. After the irrigation of that crop was completed, the sod would be replaced and a different sluice opened. Depending on the strength of the river, several sluices could be opened at the same time. Third, the man who meditates brings "forth his fruit in his season"; he is productive, bearing expected fruit at the appropriate time. It is impossible for one who reads, prays, and meditates on God's Word not to produce fruits of righteousness. He will see the work God has given him to do, and he will have the power to perform that work, and he will know where and when it is to be done in order to bless the most people and to give God the most glory. Fourth, "his leaf also shall not wither"; his religion will be regular, unsullied, and abounding with good works. Even his casual conversation and actions will point others to the greatness and goodness of God. Fifth, "whatsoever he doeth shall prosper." Because his soul is healthy and strong, extending its roots ever deeper into the Word of God, he is continually growing in grace and heavenly desires and God, in turn, is blessing the work of his hands with productivity, creativity, and expansion. Meditation is the birthplace of creativity. "For the Lord watches over all the plans and paths of godly men." [38]

God's Word and His presence are the keys to growth. That is why it is important to major in the Word. The Bible is not a textbook on economics, science, social studies, marriage, psychology; it is not a textbook about any one of those things; it is a textbook about all those things because it is written by the Creator of all things. [39] It is inspired by God and profitable to life. [40] Moses knew the ways of God and followed them in successfully leading more than a million people out of the slavery of Egypt; it is time for us to know God's ways. [41] It is when we refuse to know His Word that we are contributing to our own destruction. [42] We are limited by the knowledge in our mind. The width, the depth and the breadth of our knowledge is the foundation for the life that we live and the purpose we fulfill. Knowledge of the Word precedes holiness and obedience and shows the ways of God. [43] Theodore Roosevelt said, "A thorough knowledge of the Bible is worth more than a college education." Therefore, if we want to reach our potential, we should learn God's promises, His patterns, and obey His Word. [44, 45]

If our heart is not in it, however, we will not reach our potential. We must believe and confess with our mouth what is in our heart. Confessing God's Word will accomplish two things: (1) we will write His Word upon our heart, and (2) we will start believing what we say. [46, 47] The words coming out of our mouth will determine whether we are satisfied.

We create our world by the words we speak. We are created in the image and likeness of God. God created the universe by His spoken word. We, too, create our world by the words we speak. When we speak God's Word to the circumstances of our life, we are providing evidence that we agree with God! When we speak God's Word over our lives, we are speaking the will of God into our lives and God watches over His Word to perform it.

Agreement is the place of power. Disagreement is the place of powerlessness. When we agree with God, we bring the power of God into our circumstances to accomplish His perfect will.

Salvation comes by way of the mouth; confession, an expression of the deeply held beliefs of the heart, brings salvation into being. [48] *Soteria*, which is translated as salvation, in its root meaning describes both physical and moral rescue and safety; this implies healing, deliverance, preservation, the ministering of angels and soundness. [49] After it dawns on us that we have been truly saved and delivered, we will want to praise God and worship Him. Our heart will be filled with prayer and praise. [50]

The next step is to confess what we believe to ourselves and to others. Frequent confession focuses our mind on both what God has done for us and for our dream. It allows us to train all our mental, emotional, and physical abilities on fulfilling the dream. It allows us to start discussing with God how to reach our goal. We will find that He will lead us through the steps of gaining wisdom, developing strategy, and finally exhibiting leadership. He will also hear the petitions of our needs.

Be aware that when we talk to God about our need, He is going to talk to us about our seed. He wants us to embrace the principle of seedtime and harvest. God instituted seedtime and harvest and it will never fail. [51] As long as earth remains, no one will be able to stop God's method of seedtime and harvest. In a basic sense, seedtime and harvest has to do with the cultivation of crops: the ground is cultivated, seeds are planted, carefully watered and tended, and at the proper time crops are harvested. In a larger sense, seedtime and harvest applies to almost anything in life: planting, tending, growth, and harvest. [52] When we start planting and harvesting on a consistent and continual basis our harvest will never fail. [53] Jesus' parable of the talents, which we will consider in chapter three, not only illustrates this point in greater detail but it emphasizes that character is developed by doing things God's way. This can only be achieved through faithfulness.

## Faithfulness is the cornerstone of character

God wants us to be like Him and He wants to know that He can trust us. That is why He asks for our faithfulness, our unswerving allegiance to Him, His Word, and His guidance. Faithfulness is the proving ground of faith. It is demonstrated in three ways: (1) the care of greater things is based on our care of smaller things; (2) the care of the natural precedes the care of the spiritual; (3) our ability to care for the property of others qualifies us to care for our own. Jesus emphasized these concepts in the parable of the unjust steward or accountant. Briefly, the accountant was accused of being dishonest, and the employer told him to get his reports in order because he was being dismissed. The accountant was afraid that he would not find additional employment, so he devised a way of strengthening his network. He invited each person who owed his employer to come for an interview, during which he rewrote the debtor's contract and reduced the amount owed. "Unless you are honest in small matters," Jesus pointed out, "you won't be in large ones. If you cheat even a little, you won't be honest with greater responsibilities. If you are untrustworthy about worldly wealth, who will trust you with the true riches of heaven? And if you are not faithful with other people's money, why should you be entrusted with money of your own?" [54]

"For neither you nor anyone else can serve two masters. You will hate one and show loyalty to the other; or else the other way around, you will be enthusiastic about one and despise the other. You cannot serve both God and money." [55] Obviously the accountant was serving himself, not his employer. The point Jesus made here is that character—who we are, not who we know or what we know—determines our success. He has laid out in His Word specific guidelines to help us achieve His best. He wants to give us the kingdom, but He will do so only when we have proven that He comes first and we are willing to do things His way.

## Summary

- We are created in the image of God, possessing His nature, power, and authority.

- Building a Christ-like character is a process, not an event.

- God will never throw us into a fight that we cannot win.

- Seek God first in all things; make the pursuit of Him #1.

- We were created to manifest the glory of God; that is our purpose: To cover the earth with the glory and will of God.

- God wants us to declare His praise.

- Faith is necessary to please God.

- Diligence brings rewards, for God is a rewarder of those who diligently seek Him.

- God is constantly thinking of us and about how He can bring increase into every area of our lives.

- The kingdom of God is simply, "Doing things God's way."

- Deception is doing what we believe to be the will of God in "our way."

- Meditation is the birthplace of creativity.

- Worry is negative meditation, distracting us from focusing on the Word of God and the promises of God.

- Faithfulness is evidenced in our stewardship of God's gifts to us. It is measured from small things to large things, from the natural to the spiritual, and from the property of others to our own.

- Christlike character is your destiny.

# • CHAPTER THREE •

## GOD'S PLAN FOR MAN

Doing things God's way requires that we understand the principles by which He operates. Paul urged Timothy to study the Scriptures to show himself approved unto God. [56] At that time, the New Testament had not yet been written, so most of the patterns had to come from the Old Testament; Paul also wrote in *Corinthians* that the experiences of Israel were examples, *tupos,* to teach us not to lust after evil things as they had lusted. [57] *Tupos,* which is translated "example" in *Corinthians,* means *pattern.*

The patterns we are looking at in this chapter concern the principles by which God does His work and come from the parable of the talents. [58] Jesus began this teaching with explaining what the kingdom of God is like: "For the kingdom of heaven is as a man traveling into a far country, who called his own servants and delivered his goods to them." [59] Then He proceeded to show us how God apportions work, how He values work, and how He rules His kingdom.

Work is important to God. It existed in the garden before God created Eve; God gave Adam the responsibility of tending and keeping the Garden of Eden[60] and naming each living creature. [61] Work is a holy and sacred calling because that is where our heart is revealed and where we learn stewardship. Work is where the Word is made flesh in our lives. As faithfulness is the cornerstone of character, so is stewardship the cornerstone of faithfulness. In 1983, I was in a career crisis; I had lost my job and did not know who I wanted to be or what I wanted to do. I had grown up in a legalistic church and had a warped value system regarding money and work. After I met Dr. Cole, of the Christian Men's Network, I discovered that God does not deal with solitary topics but that everything affects everything else; in other words, "All truth is parallel." In addition to spiritual issues, the Bible addresses government, economics, science, sociology, health, and many other topics. I also learned that the Bible has a lot to say about work and money. In this chapter are some propositions that, if applied, will change our lives, the lives of our children, family, people with whom we work, and that will allow us to fulfill God's ordained destiny for our lives. Here, then, are eleven propositions that demonstrate how the kingdom of God operates.

## Proposition 1. God owns everything. [62]

"He called his own servants and delivered his goods to them." [63] We own nothing; we do not even own what we possess. We are only stewards of those things with which He has entrusted us. So we possess our bodies, but we do not own them. They are given to us by God. We possess our minds, but we do not own them. We have wives, but our wives are not our property. We have children, but we do not own them; they too are gifts from God. Everything we have—people, things, talents—everything is a gift from God. The parable says the master delivered unto his own servants all his goods. Are we not all servants of God?

God has a destiny for each of us, and this destiny is based on our gifting. We cannot imagine where God ultimately means to take us. We can know only that He will not take us to our destiny in one single exponential leap. He will take us little by little, bit by bit, day by day as we walk in obedience to His Word. He tests us, judges us, and holds us accountable just as the master in the parable held his servants accountable for the talents distributed to them. I do not know what your destiny is, but I know God is able to do exceedingly and abundantly above all that we can ask or even think. [64] I know that eyes have not seen and ears have not heard, nor has it entered into the heart of man what God has prepared for those who love him. [65] I know that His eyes go to and fro throughout the whole earth to show Himself strong on behalf of those whose hearts are perfect towards Him. [66] I know that the people that know their God shall be strong and carry out great exploits. [67] I know that God's destiny for us is bigger than anything we have ever dreamed.

Fellowship with God is to steward properly what He has given us. The essence of the kingdom, then, is to discover, develop and dedicate

God's gifts to us, refining and dedicating them to the glory of God. David expressed it best, "The earth is the LORD's, and everything in it, the world and all its people belong to him" (Psalm 24:1, NLT).

## Proposition 2. God has given us something.

"He called his own servants and delivered his goods to them." [68] We all have received something from God that is unique to us. All of us are created special; we have something that no one else has, an anointing, a talent, ability, a gift, a spiritual endowment. What has God given us? He has given us a mind, a body, some of us a spouse and children. He has given some of us property, relationships and gifts. There are no second-class citizens in the kingdom of God.

God's plan for our lives shows us our destiny. The first people in the congregation of Moses who were filled with the Holy Spirit were not the priests or men of God, but craftsmen and artisans—the workers and laborers—men who had been commissioned by God to perform a particular service. Think about it. When we discover the one thing that we can do better than almost anybody else, that is God's plan for our life. Because we are negative by nature, we tend to focus more on things that we cannot do than on the things that we can. We focus on our weaknesses more than on our strengths. This awareness of negative things, for most of us, probably started in the first grade when we brought home our first report card. "Mama, Mama, Mama," we cried, "look at my report card!" There were some good grades, some average grades, but maybe one bad grade. Out of all those grades, which one did she want to talk about the most? The bad grade; the weakness. Throughout the rest of our lives, we have probably been addressing our weaknesses, trying to develop and strengthen them.

God has given each of us at least one strength or ability that we can do better than ten thousand other people can do. Satan, however, does not want us to recognize our strengths. That is why he tries to blind us to both our gift and God's way of handling that gift; that is one of his major deceptions. Sadly, we are more aware of the things we cannot do than we are of the things we do well. For example, if we were asked to list our strengths, we probably would write only four or five. Statistics show, however, that if we were asked to list our weaknesses, we would write fifteen or twenty. Therein lies the first reason we do not fulfill our destiny: we focus on our weaknesses. We think, *Well, if I focus on my weaknesses, everything is going to be all right.* Focusing all our time on improving weaknesses will only make us average. Interestingly, the world wants us to become part of the group, the mediocre ones; focusing on weaknesses will accomplish that. But God did not make us to be average; He made us for excellence. We are His workmanship, a unique work of art, created in Christ Jesus unto good works, in which God has ordained that we should walk. [69] That is why He wants us to focus on our strengths, to find excellence in the one thing we can do better than anyone else.

Another mistake we make is that instead of developing the gift or ability we set it aside and take it for granted. We think, *I can already do that so I will set it aside and develop this weakness or find something else to do.* We take God's gift for granted and do not develop it; we don't even appreciate it. At that moment, we have wasted an opportunity, because we have set aside God's plan and are following our own plan. When we were in school, improving weaknesses was appropriate, but once we enter our career path, God wants us to build on our strengths.

A good way to begin is with a self-inventory, using these questions:

1. What do I do well?

2. What do I enjoy doing?

3. What do other people say I do well?

4. What do I have opportunities to do now?

5. In what area in my past have I experienced rapid learning?

6. In what areas have I experienced glimpses of excellence?

The answers to these questions will reveal God's plan. Do not worry about weaknesses. They can be overcome by partnering with people who are strong in the areas where we are weak. I have discovered my gift and I try to focus on it because I am heading for my destiny. For example, I own five corporations but I do not like preparing and filing tax returns and quarterly reports, so I have hired an accountant who loves all those details. When I dump all those boxes on his desk, he just shivers with delight and I say, "Thank God, for accountants!" When my wife tells me a faucet is leaking, I tell her to call a plumber. I can probably fix the faucet, but I can make so much more money doing what I do best.

The Scriptures say that a man's gift makes room for him and brings him before great men. [70] The one thing we do better than anyone else is God's plan for our destiny. If we find God's gift, develop it, refine it, and dedicate it to the glory of God, we will fulfill God's plan. When He returns He will ask, like the master in the parable, "What have you done with what I gave you?"

## Proposition 3. We are not created equal.

"To one he gave five talents, to another two, and to another one." [71] God gives different gifts to different men. God did not make anyone else like us, nor has He gifted us the same. When we recognize the fact that we do not have to compete with anyone and that we can just be ourselves, it allows us to be everything God wants us to be. In the kingdom, there is no competing and no complaining. We have within us everything necessary to achieve the destiny God has laid out for us. If we focus on our gifting, we can live a life of excellence.

Excellence is not being THE best. Excellence is being the best that YOU can be.

## Proposition 4. Our future is found in our past.

"He gave to each according to his own ability." [72] Something in the past of these three servants in the parable qualified them for the number of talents that were left with them. The master was testing them again to see how they would handle his affairs. Gifts vary in quantity based on our handling of previous gifts. Diligent stewardship shows maturity and qualifies us for more responsibility. When we prove to God that we will handle the gifts He has given us diligently and responsibly, He will always give us more. The experiences of our past qualify us for our ordained destiny.

"All experience is an arch to build upon." —Henry Adams

## Proposition 5. We must invest to increase.

"He who had received five talents went and traded with them, and made another five talents. And likewise he who had received two." [73] Talents are of greater value than we usually imagine. In the parable of the talents, the master gave the first man five talents, the second man two talents and the third man one talent. A talent is approximately 6,000 denarii. One denarius was equal to a day's wage. In today's economy, one talent equals $600,000; two talents equal $1.2 million; five talents equal $3 million. Like the man in the parable who went on a journey, God is a businessman who has entrusted us with His goods, and when He returns, He expects an increase on what He has given us. In order for us to experience increase, we have to invest the talent. We have to put it at risk. We have to be willing to fail. We have to take a chance. We even have to trust in God. We have to get out of our comfort zone and go beyond the map. We may have to do some things we have never done before so that we can develop the gift He has given us.

The rewards that we experience are based on our faithfulness, not on how many talents we possess. The man with the two talents received the same reward as the man with five talents; they both doubled their talents and brought the master 100 percent return on his investment. We do not use the talent to compete or compare ourselves but rather to fulfill our destiny. We must prove ourselves faithful at our present level to qualify for the next. Thomas Jefferson said, "He does most in God's great world who does his best in his own little world." To acquire more talent, we must be faithful with the talent we now possess. To acquire more financial resources, we must prove ourselves faithful with the financial resources we now possess. Whatever desire we possess, we must first prove ourselves faithful with what we have now. This principle of the kingdom applies to every area of life. Faith is sometimes spelled, R-I-S-K.

If we want to increase in any area, we have to give. The principle of the kingdom is give so that it may be returned to us in good measure, pressed down, shaken all together and running over. [74] The context of this statement is about forgiveness, but it applies to us spiritually, physically, and emotionally because "All truth is parallel." If we want love, we give love. If we want wisdom, we give the wisdom we have away. If we want 20-inch biceps, what do we have to do? In order to gain strength, we must give strength. When God finds someone He can trust to share his resources with others, then He gives that person more resources. Fulfilling our destiny and our potential is not about us; it is always about other people. We are created in the image and likeness of God; therefore, we are to share His character and attributes. The Scriptures tell us that God so loved the world that He gave. [75] If He gave, then we should give. Whatever we give, God will give us more because we are conduits for His will in the earth.

A person will reap exactly what he sows (Galatians 6:7).

## Proposition 6. Embrace delayed gratification.

"But he who had received one went and dug in the ground, and hid his lord's money. After a long time the lord of those servants came and settled accounts with them." [76] Being gone a long time implies seedtime and harvest, and risk and return. Just because it takes a long time to see an increase in an investment does not mean that the increase is not coming. When we plant a seed in the ground, we do not go out tomorrow to find Jack's beanstalk reaching to the sky. It takes time for a harvest. This is true in every area: with money, talent, virtually everything. Once we have done the will of God, we must wait for the increase. Waiting involves expectation, prayer, praise, and being content with simple things. Many young people get married thinking that in a few years they should be at the same lifestyle their parents had after thirty years of marriage, so they burden themselves with debt, which leads to financial stress that, in turn, causes marital stress. This immature attitude regarding material things will probably shorten their marriage.

Endurance is a key element in embracing delayed gratification. Waiting is the test. God gives us a talent and He wants to see what we will do with it. Are we developing the talent and bringing increase to the kingdom? Are we taking it to the workplace, operating in excellence, being diligent, being disciplined, doing our best, bringing reward back to the Master so the kingdom of God can be advanced? The Bible says that we are to be kings and priests unto God for glory and dominion. In the Old Testament, the kings went to battle, vanquished the enemies of God and established dominion. In today's economy, the marketplace is the battlefield. If we are businessmen, we are like the kings of old and God expects us to go into the marketplace and establish economic dominion, because when the church has economic dominion, then she is establishing the kingdom of God in the earth.

We must also embrace delayed gratification in our personal financial integrity. God will not trust us with greater financial resources if we cannot manage what we have now. He who is faithful in little is also faithful in much. [77] God will not trust us with true riches in His kingdom until we can handle unrighteous mammon. Some thirty-nine or so years ago, I was an apprentice pressman for a printing company. I remember that the owner of the company would walk through the door wearing a nice suit and I would think, *Wow! I wonder what it would be like to own my own business? I'll bet that suit cost $500. Man, I'll bet he makes $100,000 a year!* I was making $6,000 a year, and if I had not managed my money, stayed out of debt, paid my tithes, and shown God that I could manage my resources, He would never have entrusted me with more.

Jesus taught that we must be faithful in the small things to qualify ourselves for more. Then he spoke about money, saying that if we were not faithful with our money we could not be trusted with the real riches of His kingdom. Going a step further, He pronounced that if we were not faithful with another man's property, we were not qualified to have our own. [78] If we cannot tithe on $50,000 a year, we would never be able to tithe on $500,000 a year. There is no sense in our even wondering and dreaming about making $500,000 a year, because God is never going to allow us to have it if we cannot tithe on what we already make. Scripture says, "The tithe is the Lord's." The tithe belongs to God; it is not ours. When we pay our tithe, we have not given God anything; all we have done is decide not to steal from Him. We have not given God anything until we have given an offering.

Money proves so many things about our lives. In many ways, how we handle it and what we do with it, it is the proving ground of character. *Staying out of debt* means not taking on any more debt. It means getting to the place where we buy something only if we can pay cash for it. If we are encumbered with debt, we cannot take advantage of opportunities that come our way. We do not have to pray for opportunities; they will come. We must focus on being ready to capture them, staying out of debt is one way to be ready. What will happen, though not overnight, is that we will show God that He can trust us with financial resources and He will then give us more.

Another obstacle to embracing delayed gratification is the desire to *look* blessed instead of *being* blessed. Some people run up debt and live beyond their means, which creates financial pressure in the home and in the family, and eventually leads to divorce. Faithful men live below their means. I learned years ago that if I could not pay for something not to buy it. The only credit cards I ever had were those I had to pay off in thirty days, so they became money management tools. If we focus on getting out of debt, we will eventually get to the place where we will not owe anyone anything but to love him. I know, because I am there now.

God is no respecter of persons, [79] but He is a respecter of obedience, faith, and diligent adherence to His principles. While it does not happen overnight, the increase will come when we sow and develop our gift and take it to the workplace and operate in excellence so that God receives the glory. With God's wisdom, His power, and His ability, we will be able to solve problems the unbeliever cannot solve because we are identified with

Christ. In the parable, the master gave to one man five talents, to another two, and to another one, as a test to see what they would do with it. God wants to multiply abundance in our lives, but we control whether He can do so. When we are faithful with using our gift to bring Him increase, He can multiply our rewards; but when we are unfaithful, He takes from us and gives to another who will be faithful.

"So don't get tired of doing what is good. Don't get discouraged and give up, for we will reap a harvest of blessing at the appropriate time" (Galatians 6:9, NLT).

## Proposition 7. God rewards faithfulness.

"I have gained ... more talents besides them."[80] We are only accountable for what He has given us; we are not accountable for anything else. God is actually more interested in what He can do in and through us than in what He can do for us. If He can do something in us and through us, then we can do something for other people. He knows that to be a blessing to others, we have to be blessed and He is perfectly willing to bestow on us a double portion as a reward for our faithfulness. Faithfulness precedes blessing. Both faithful servants, in the parable of the talents, received the same reward. The master said to them, "You have been faithful over a little; you can now be faithful over much." God does not reward us based on the number of gifts we have, He rewards us on our faithfulness in using those gifts. When we are faithful, we qualify ourselves for more. These servants were given twice as much. That is what God wants in our lives: He wants us to have a double portion. "Unless you are faithful in small matters, you won't be faithful in large ones. If you cheat even a little, you won't be honest with greater responsibilities" (Luke 16:10, NLT).

## Proposition 8. God expects interest on His loan.

"Well done, good and faithful servant."[81] God is a businessman looking for a return on His investment. He did not give us the talent to hold and look at; He gave it to us to use.

God assigns responsibilities and authority to those who will properly steward His investment. In the parable, which Jesus said would show us what the kingdom of God is like, the master gave each servant the number of talents He thought the servant could manage. Both the five-talent and the two-talent servants doubled their talents and the master was pleased upon his return. Their faithfulness led to added responsibility.

But the servant who received only one talent hid his talent and, upon the master's return, accused the master of being unfair and harsh. This man had been assigned the same task as the others, but he acted as though, by returning the original talent, he was fulfilling that task. He failed to reckon with the principles of return and reward, which says that to whom much is given much is required. [82] The principle of reward states that more shall be given to him who has. [83] "Much is required from those to whom much is given, and much more is required from those to whom much more is given" (Luke 12:48, NLT).

## Proposition 9. Fear is the enemy of faith.

"I was afraid, and went and hid your talent in the ground." [84] Fear is the biggest obstacle to fulfilling our destiny. Fear and faith have the same definition; both focus on something that has not happened yet. Faith dwells on the positive; fear, on the negative. We are told that one man in the parable hid his talent because he was afraid. What did he fear? He might have been afraid of success. Many people fear success. They do not want to go to the next level because they might have to leave their friends behind. This often happens, but we must understand that not everyone will be happy for us when we go to the next level financially. We must decide whether we want to be powerful or popular. We cannot be both. When we go to the next level, however, God will give us a new group of intimate friendships, people who share the same vision, mission, values, responsibilities, and who are able to encourage us to go higher. When we go to a higher level of living, we must be willing to leave some intimate friendships behind.

This reminds me of the old Indian story of a boy who found an eagle's egg and put it in a prairie chicken's nest. The young eagle hatched and found himself surrounded by prairie chickens; hence, he thought he was a prairie chicken. He pecked at the dirt, ate bugs and worms and scratched around. One day he looked up and saw an eagle soaring majestically in the sky.

"Wow! what an awesome sight!" he said, "What is that?"

One of his prairie chicken friends told him that it was an eagle, the greatest of all of God's creation in birds. "The greatest bird there is. Isn't that awesome?"

"Yeah," said the little eagle, "I sure would like to be an eagle."

"Well, you are not. You will always be a prairie chicken."

There will always be people who try to keep us at the level of mediocrity. So long as we stop thinking about increase in our life, mediocrity is what we will accept; but when we realize that God made us for excellence, we will rise above that and go to the next level. We will have a new level of understanding and we will have a new level of intimate friendships.

If you accept someone else's philosophy, that is a rationalization to justify their failure, then you accept their failure. If you accept their failure then you have allowed them to create your world for you. As Dr. Edwin Louis Cole taught me, "Don't let someone else make decisions for you and in so doing create your world for you, because they will always create it too small." Others may fear failure. "Champions are not those who never fail; champions are those who never quit." I have failed at many things but I have learned that I must never quit. The Bible says that if a righteous man falls seven times, he will rise again. [85] We have not failed until we quit. Someone said, "You don't drown by falling in water, you drown by staying there." When the horse throws us off, we dust off our pants and get back on, and ride that horse. All success is born out of failure. *Fortune* magazine conducted a study several years ago and found that the one hundred wealthiest Americans that ever lived, averaged failing seven times each. Thomas Edison failed 10,000 times before he invented the lead storage battery. Benjamin Franklin, when asked, replied, "My secret to success is that I am not afraid to fail." The average entrepreneur in the United States fails 3.2 times before he makes it. Most businessmen that I know of are just ex-failures that finally made it. There is nothing to fear from failure because we have nothing to hide.

"His lord answered and said to him, you wicked and lazy servant!" [86] Had this servant put his money to risk and failed, I believe the master would have given him another chance. But he was afraid to take the risk and from his failure we learn a valuable lesson. The gift that God gave us is not ours, it is His and He expects interest on what is loaned to us. That interest is our recognizing the gift and developing it and using it for economic empowerment so that we can establish dominion of the kingdom of God in the world.

"Our greatest glory is not in never failing, but in rising every time we fall." —Confucius

## Proposition 10. Law of use and disuse, increase and decline.

We must use our talent or lose it. The master took away the one talent from the servant who had buried it and gave it to the servant who had gained ten talents. I can see people questioning whether such an action was right. *Why would he do such a thing?* they ask. Because the master was a businessman, and he had entrusted these men with his resources. He looked at the man who hid the talent in the ground instead of at least putting it in the bank and thought, *I'm not going through that again. I will give it to the man who knows what to do with it.* Likewise, God does not suffer mediocrity. He does not judge us for trying and failing; He judges us for not trying. That is why the talent was taken from the slothful servant and given to the one with ten talents. He wants us to have abundance. [87]

God has given us a talent. What are we doing with it? One of these days God will return and ask, "What did you do with the mechanical ability I gave you? What did you do with the musical ability I gave you? With that mathematical ability I gave you? What did you do with that precious gift that I gave you?" Is He going to say, "Well done, good and faithful servant"? Or is He going to cast us into outer darkness where there is weeping and gnashing of teeth? God will hold us accountable for the stewardship of the resources He has entrusted to us.

The enemy wants to keep us blind to our gifting; he wants to keep us in mediocrity and poverty. He deceives us by telling us that we are just businessmen, therefore, we must not be very spiritual. This is the value system known as dualism, which teaches that spirit is good and matter is evil. Under this system, if we really want to be good, we must be spiritual and not embrace material things. Under this system, we who are called to the business world and not to ministry are made to feel second rate. We wonder why God did not love us enough to make us preachers. In this parable, God is telling us that our work is our ministry and that God has identified with the material realm and will judge us by our stewardship of the resources He has given us. There is no dualism with God, because we demonstrate our spiritual growth by proving ourselves in the natural, material realm.

The earth is God's, [88] and He has commissioned us to take dominion over it and every living thing on it. [89] If we take the resources He has given us and manage them by biblical principles, He will give us increase: we will bring glory to God.

The way we bring glory to God is by doing things God's way. The Bible says that the priest would handle the glory of God and the kings would establish dominion. Kings in today's economy are the business people of the church. Sadly, we kings have not been fulfilling our commission. Although God wants us to establish the kingdom of God on earth, it will not happen until we have economic influence. Ecclesiastes says that money answers all things. [90] Faith moves heaven, but money moves the earth. The church needs financial resources to do the work of God on this earth. God anoints the business community to steward His resources in a Christ-like way to bring resources into the church so that the will of God can cover the earth. Our work is just as valuable to the kingdom as that of the man who stands behind the pulpit and preaches. Actually, I think it more valuable because God made more of us. The preacher, the pastor, the apostle, the prophet, the evangelist cannot fulfill God's commission and cover the earth with the will of God alone. That responsibility has to take place in the workplace and in everything we do.

"Do you see a man who excels in his work? He will stand before kings; He will not stand before unknown men" (Proverbs 22:29, NKJV).

## Proposition 11. God wants us to have abundance.

"Therefore take the talent from him, and give it to him who has ten talents." [91] God has given us something very special; we already have all we need to establish dominion. We have at least one talent and the only way we are going to increase it is to develop and use it. It is the Father's good pleasure to give us the kingdom, [92] but He will not do so unless we prove ourselves faithful; because the reward of the trustworthy is more trust, and if He cannot trust us with one talent, He will not give us any more. The eyes of the Lord go to and fro throughout the earth to show himself strong on behalf of those whose hearts are perfect toward Him. [93] He has given us an anointing and He is testing us to see whether we will be faithful in using that anointing, because He cannot give us any more unless we bring Him increase. If we hide the talent He has given, we are rebelling against Him and sinning. For to know to do good and not do it is a sin. [94] If we prove to be unfaithful, God will take from us and give to the servant who has proven faithful.

Not only will we lose what He has given us if we do not steward it properly, we will be cast into outer darkness where there is weeping and gnashing of teeth. [95] I do not know if that means hell, but I do know that it is not a good place. Some theologians say that we will not lose our justification but that we are losing our place at the banquet table, that we will not be in the limelight but that we will be in darkness agonizing over missed opportunities. We had a gift from God and did not develop it or use it; therefore, we missed God's plan for our life.

Men and women all around the world ask, "What is God's plan for my life?" Proverbs says that a man's gift will make room for him and bring him before great men. [96] We are not talking about money but about talent, the gifting, anointing, or endowment that God gives us. When we develop that gift, it will promote us and bring us before great men. It will make room for us. If the enemy can keep us in the dark regarding our gifting, then he can keep us in poverty and mediocrity, he can keep us from fulfilling the destiny God has planned for us. Jesus came that we might have life and have it more abundantly. [97] *Perissos* means "super abundance, excessive overflowing surplus, more than enough." I do not mean to imply that all of us will be millionaires or multi-millionaires, although we might; I am simply saying that we have to be blessed to become a blessing to others. The Scriptures say that God wants us to prosper and be in good health even as our souls prosper. [98] Our soul includes our mind, our will, our emotions, and our thought life.

Not only has God given us the gift and the ability to develop it, He has also given us an anointing. [99] Many people think the anointing is only for preachers, but according to 1 John 2:20, if we are believers, we have the anointing; verse 27 states that the anointing abides within us and we know all things. [100] This means the Holy Spirit will lead us into areas of knowledge that we have never experienced so that we have answers to problems the unbeliever does not have. Most of us spend at least forty hours a week at work and we take the Holy Spirit with us. What differences are we making on our job because of the anointing?

### The blessings of the Lord cause stress

We cannot be effective and not be controversial; nor can we expect everyone to like and support us. We have to choose between being powerful or popular. There are two kinds of people: those who do things and those who criticize people who do things. This new level of living will transform us into people who do things and this transformation will require us to leave behind those who are jealous of our success and who are not happy for us.

Economic empowerment is more about the gift than the giving. No matter how much we give, if we do not understand that we are gifted, there is no room for us. God has never created anything without a gift, not a man, woman, child, or even a plant. God has a destiny for each of us and He has given us the ability to fulfill it. The enemy attacks us with low self-esteem when he wants to curse us with poverty, because when self-esteem is low we do not realize we have a contribution to make. Consequently, we will hide our gift and not seek to multiply it. We think if we cannot offer the same as another person, we have no gift. This, of course, is simply not true. We are unique and must refuse to imitate others. Each of us is chosen by God for a specific reason; no one else can fulfill His will as completely. Race, social status, education has little to do with economic empowerment. We can refuse to be broke and live in poverty. We can work our way out and create our own opportunities. To do this we must change our lifestyle. Wealth is multi-generational; God blesses three generations at a time. For example, Abraham, Isaac and Jacob came under the same covenant blessing. Families are blessed because someone in the family dug his way out of poverty, but this cannot be done if we are high, drunk, frustrated, angry, depressed or if we cannot stand delayed gratification. To follow our destiny, we must stay out of debt and become investors not consumers. To go from level to level, we must invest in ourselves and believe in our gift and our uniqueness. God has commissioned us to rule. He has authorized us to have dominion over everything on the earth. The Lord has anointed us to be leaders. God has ordained us to be either a priest or a king. In the next chapter, we will learn to differentiate between them.

## Summary

- God owns everything; we own nothing. We do not own what we possess; we are merely stewards of those possessions.

- Work was important to God in Eden before Eve was ever created. Work is where the Word of God is revealed to the world.

- Our destiny is inextricably tied to our gifting.

- God is a gradualist; He is not in a hurry.

- God's plan for our life far surpasses our fondest dreams. He will not show it to us lest it frighten us.

- Fellowship with God is when we properly and faithfully steward the gifts He has entrusted to us.

- God has given us something very special— a talent, an ability, a special endowment that is uniquely ours.

- There are no second-class citizens in the kingdom of God.

- Reaching our fullest potential in life is found when we focus and improve our strengths, not our weaknesses.

- God wants us to focus on our strengths; the world wants us to focus on our weaknesses.

- If the enemy can get us to focus on our weaknesses and neglect our strengths, he can keep us from fulfilling our potential in life.

- In the kingdom of God, there is no competing, no comparing, and no complaining.

- Our future is found in the experiences of our past. No one in the world was better qualified to lead the children of Israel out of Egypt than Moses, because of his experiences in the wilderness and Pharaoh's court.

- We must invest to increase.

- Increase only comes when we are patient and expectant in waiting

- God is no respecter of person. He is a respecter of faith and diligence.

- Faithfulness precedes blessing.

- The rewards we receive are based on our faithfulness.

- The man who is faithful in small things will also be faithful in larger things.

- To go to the next level in any area of life, we must be willing to leave our old friends behind.

- Champions are not those who never fail. Champions are those who never quit.

- We have not failed until we quit; therefore, a key principle for success is that we never quit. NEVER!

- Most successful entrepreneurs are ex-failures who just got mad.

- God will never judge us for failing. God will judge us for not trying.

- It is a sin when we know to do something good and we don't do it. Therefore, if we know how to prosper, which is good, and we don't do it we have sinned.

- Once we have done the will of God, we must wait for the increase.

- Fear is the biggest obstacle to fulfilling our destiny.

- Christlike character is your destiny.

# CHAPTER FOUR

## DOMINION COMMISSION

Knowing God is not an event; it is a process. It is something we do every day, and our relationship with Him changes constantly, as we know Him better and more intimately. Knowing God entails total commitment and some sacrifice; it means going to the cross, renewing our minds, and transforming our lives in alignment with His Word. These steps are necessary for us to fulfill our God-ordained destiny, whose purpose, according to Isaiah 43:7, is to bring glory to God. [101] We are not made for mediocrity; we were made for God's glory and to establish His dominion on the earth.

### Dominion commission

Many people are not familiar with the dominion commission of the Old Testament, found in Genesis 1:26-28. In this commission, God says we were created in the image of God and in His likeness and that we are to be fruitful and to multiply, to replenish the earth and have dominion over it. [102] It is obvious, however, when we look around that man does not truly have dominion. The Bible tells us that man handed off his claim to dominion to Satan at the Fall. Since then the great struggle between good and evil has touched all our lives. God, through giving His Son, Jesus, redeemed fallen man and restored him to his rightful place of rulership, but Satan actively works to deceive man.

Who then is in power? Christ or Satan? After the resurrection, the disciples met Jesus on a mountain in Galilee; most of them worshipped Him when they saw Him, but some doubted. Jesus then explained to them that He is the rightful possessor of all power and gave them the Great Commission of the New Testament, "All authority has been given to Me in heaven and on earth. Go therefore and make disciples of all the nations, baptizing them in the name of the Father and of the Son and of the Holy Spirit, teaching them to observe all things that I have commanded you; and lo, I am with you always, even to the end of the age." [103] Yet Satan continues to war against mankind. He tries to get us to accept mediocrity, to be subservient to all sorts of addictions, and afraid to stand up to him and his minions. Despite the fact that Jesus Christ "has made us kings and priests to His God and Father, to Him be glory and dominion forever and ever." [104]

One of the purposes of this book is to study the Old Testament to discover the patterns in which God gives us principles to live by, promises to believe in, examples to follow and commandments to obey. In the Old Testament there was a pattern for divine teamwork, by which God used the two primary governments in Israel to advance the kingdom. Israel had two branches of government: priests and kings. Kings were to establish dominion—in the government, in the military, in the marketplace and in the community. Originally, the king had a twofold duty: to lead the people to battle in time of war, and to execute judgment and justice during both war and peace. Besides being commander-in-chief of the army, supreme judge, and absolute master of the populace, he had the power to impose taxes and exact personal service and labor. He was considered to be vicegerent, administrative deputy, of Jehovah. [105]

The priests were primarily responsible for the glory of God in the tabernacle, in the temple, in the community. Their chief duties were to watch over the altar of burnt-offerings and to keep the fire going day and night perpetually; to offer up prayers, thanksgiving, and sacrifices; to perform the myriad duties of the tabernacle or, later, the temple; to teach the children the laws of God; to educate and civilize the people; and to act as a court of appeals in the more difficult criminal or civil cases. The priests' duties focused on two-way communications between God and man; they became both man's representatives in "things pertaining to God" and God's representatives to man in terms of vision, guidance, and instruction.

In both cases, the king and the priest were called out and anointed by God to serve in his capacity. It seems that the calling and the anointing recognized the innate gifts and talents of the man. At that point, the work became his ministry to God; his work became a form of worship. "Worship" derives from the Old English word *woerth* meaning "worth" and the suffix "-ship" which establishes the "quality or condition of" something—in this case, "the quality or condition of worth." Anything you do that establishes God's worth in your life is worship. When you attend a meeting that establishes God's worth in your life, that attendance is a form of worship. When you read your Bible, or pray, or study the Bible with your children, or attend church, if God's worth is established in your life those actions are forms of worship. When you go to work with the mandate from God to establish dominion, recognizing that you have been created for excellence and that you are God's masterpiece; when you recognize your gifting and anointing and take those to the marketplace and God gives you new ideas, innovations, strategies, and techniques so that He can transit the wealth of the world into the church, that too is a form of worship.

It is necessary for us to get beyond the idea that to please God and to serve Him effectively, we must be preachers. This simply is not true; the work of the king in the Old Testament was just as vital and necessary as the work of the priests. Since life is lived on two levels, public and private, we all have opportunity to function as both priest and king. In private, kings function in intercessory roles as priests to their families. In private, priests function in kingship roles to provide for and lead their families. In our public lives, each of us is either a king or a priest; one calling dominates the other. Because of our gifts, we will be predominately a king or predominately a priest, and will minister in the area of our anointing. Like me, you may be anointed for business, anointed as a king.

It seems obvious that more believers will be anointed as kings than as priests, because the priesthood did not dominate kingship in the Old Testament. Of twelve tribes in Israel, only one tribe functioned in the priesthood. That tribe, Levi, was the smallest tribe. For every Levite, there were twenty-seven other Israelites that were warriors, conquerors, soldiers, businessmen, bankers, attorneys, physicians; all of them were taking dominion over their world and providing for the worship of Jehovah. No wonder the neighboring nations feared Israel and made statements like, "Their God fights for them and against us!"

## The kingdom and the church, however, are not synonymous

In Genesis, you saw that we have been commissioned to conquer; God created us in His image and then told us to be fruitful and multiply and establish dominion over the earth. Even the infant church was called out and anointed for dominion. Jesus called His disciples and followers from every walk of life; this group formed the first *ekklesia*, "the called out ones, the elected ones." *Ekklesia* was used in Hellenistic and Roman societies for the body of citizens who gathered to discuss the affairs of state; this body ruled over civic affairs. The history of the term explains why the Roman Empire considered the church to be such a threat. Rome knew the church was not a weak, cowering minority that would cave in at the first persecution. She knew the church had real power and influence, and that the *ekklesia* lifted a standard of righteousness that made Rome's decadence seem ragged and filthy. That is why the persecutions were stepped up; Rome was terrified that Christianity might take over her world.

Sadly, the church has lost a sense of its calling, anointing, and power. We are overdeveloped in the priesthood and underdeveloped in kingship. We have forgotten that not all were called to be priests in the Old Testament, in the New Testament, or in modern society. We have forgotten that we are commissioned to conquer. We have forgotten that there must be cooperation between the kings and priests to bring economic empowerment and dominion. The kingdom will be established, I believe, only when teamwork between the two is restored.

This teamwork will be restored only when we recognize that the difference between ecclesiastical and vocational callings rests only in focus, not in anointing. The anointing for business is the same as the anointing for ministry, and business positions are equivalent to that of the biblical elders. One of my mentors, Dennis Peacocke, taught me that we have an ecclesiastical calling and a vocational calling. The following chart demonstrates this:

Apostle    =   CEO

Prophet    =   Marketing strategist; visionary

Evangelist  =   Sales manager

Pastor     =   Human Resources and personnel

Teacher    =   Writer of manuals, policies and procedures; systems managers

Further, businessmen should have the same character requirements as the biblical elders: "blameless, husband of one wife, temperate, sober-minded, of good behavior, hospitable, able to teach; not given to wine, not violent, not greedy for money, but gentle, not quarrelsome, not covetous; one who rules his own house well, having his children in submission with all reverence; not a novice." [106, 107] Additionally, people should be employed according to their spiritual callings and gifts. Even then, problems and obstacles will distract and blur our focus.

## Destiny is surrounded by problems and obstacles

Most of our problems come from either ignorance or disobedience, which is the source of sin. Take a look at Israel. After forty years of wilderness survival, they were camped on the verge of the Promised Land, but because the spies saw some giants in the land, they rebelled against God and refused to enter. They wailed; they cried all night. They murmured against their leaders and threatened to return to Egyptian slavery because they felt betrayed. Joshua, Moses' understudy, and Caleb, the other spy with a positive report, promised, "If the Lord delights in us, then He will bring us into this land and give it to us, 'a land which flows with milk and honey.' Only do not rebel against the Lord, nor fear the people of the land, for they are our bread; their protection has departed from them, and the Lord is with us. Do not fear them." And the people repented and marched into the land? Wrong! They demanded that Joshua and Caleb be stoned! Israel had flunked and passed many tests since their departure from Egypt, but they balked at this test because of fear. And fear led to rebellion, which is sin. They failed to realize that problems are the proving ground of faith; solving problems is the test for more power.

Power and destiny, however, come through incremental problem solving. One of the biggest problems is premature promotion or inheritance. The prodigal son received a premature inheritance and, according to Jesus, he immediately left home and spent it "with riotous living" [108] *Riotous* certainly means wasteful, but it does not necessarily mean, as so many have thought, dissolute, loose morals or conduct. It would seem that the prodigal's immaturity prevented his properly managing his inheritance. It is for this reason that we must not fall into the trap of promoting potential, which is generally untried and immature, instead of character.

God promotes character, not talent. He is more concerned with our level of faithfulness than He is with our education, our pedigree, or our social status. God is searching for men and women He can trust, because the reward of the trustworthy is more trust. When we approach problems positively and offensively, instead of negatively and defensively, then we are living examples of faithfulness and we show an understanding that God is ultimately in control of our destiny.

Dennis Peacocke of Strategic Christian Services differentiates between wealth and riches in his position that wealth and riches are not synonymous. Problems reveal our character; they allow the world to see what is inside of us, to test our mettle. Adversity does not make the man; it reveals whom he really is. Problems draw from us courage, creativity, discipline, diligence, knowledge, maturity, tenacity, perseverance, wisdom, and spiritual gifts. Problems cause us to focus on our strengths instead of our weaknesses. It is through the revelation of our character that we discover our wealth.

## Wealth and riches are not synonymous

It is important to understand, up front, that wealth and riches are not synonymous. The differences between wealth and riches are threefold. First, riches are something you have; wealth is something you are. *Chayil*, the Hebrew word sometimes translated wealth, has varied meanings: "strength, power, might, efficiency, wealth, valor, force, an army, upper class." [109] Under the first four meanings, strength, power, might, efficiency, this word signified "the ability to effect or produce something." [110] Under wealth, it demonstrates one's ability and his possessions; if it is used with the words "to do or make," it means "to become wealthy or to make wealth." [111] Under the valor usage, it means "the ability to do a job well" or "the ability to conduct oneself well in battle and to be loyal to one's commander." Sometimes it can mean "army, in the sense of a combination of many individuals who, as members of an army, are distributed to perform certain functions." Finally, it can refer to the influential and wealthy people of a society.

David, the warrior king, recognized this in Psalm 144:1, "Blessed be the Lord my Rock, who trains my hands for war, and my fingers for battle." [112] So did his son, Solomon, who was a man of peace and an extremely rich man, "The blessings of the Lord makes one rich, and he adds no sorrow with it." [113] Who we are is also tied to the word *radah*, translated dominion, which means "to tread down, subjugate; specifically, to crumble off, to prevail against, to rule over." This refers us back to our earliest commission to establish dominion over the earth and over every living thing upon the earth. [114]

Second, wealth passes through death; riches will not. Riches are temporal, while wealth is eternal. It has been said that who we are is God's gift to us but what we make of ourselves is our gift to Him. Riches will burn off, but our character will remain.

Third, riches are a resource that God uses to empower those who create wealth. When God is our source, there is no idolatry because nothing comes between Him and us. When we view things or money as the source or solution to our problems, we enter into idolatry. For example, alcoholics see alcohol as the solution to their problems; drug addicts look to the drugs; and many of us look to money as the solution to our problems. In each of these cases, dependence on something other than God leads us into idolatry. "In Romans 1:22-25, idolatry, the sin of the mind against God (Ephesians 2:3), and immorality, sins of the flesh, are associated, and are traced to lack of the acknowledgment of God and of gratitude to Him. An idolater is a slave to the depraved ideas his idols represent (Galatians 4:8, 9), and thereby, to divers lusts (Titus 3:3)." [115] Idolatry can only be broken by the power of God and the acknowledgment that our wealth comes from God.

This wealth comes in the form of His character attributes: wisdom, courage, honor, understanding, discipline, hope, and faithfulness. When we conform our character to His, we possess these attributes, each of which leads to riches. Incremental problem solving adds other skills: relational skills, spiritual knowledge, understanding and sound judgment. Only after we possess His character are we able to exercise dominion as commissioned because ultimately the battles and the victories are not ours but His. David expressed this succinctly throughout the Psalms: "Bless the Lord who is my immovable Rock. He gives me strength and skill in battle." [116] Again, "And they did not gain possession of the land by their own sword, nor did their own arm save them; but it was Your right hand, Your arm, and the light of Your countenance, because You favored them." [117] Or what about this promise: "Through God we will do valiantly, for it is He who shall tread down our enemies." [118]

Daniel, the Jewish slave who was elevated to be the advisor to the King of Babylon, gratefully acknowledged God's part in his successes. "Those who do wickedly against the covenant he shall corrupt with flattery; but the people who know their God shall be strong, and carry out great exploits." [119] So also did the writer of *Hebrews:* "For God is not unfair. How can he forget your hard work for him, or forget the way you used to show your love for him—and still do—by helping his children? And we are anxious that you keep right on loving others as long as life lasts, so that you will get your full reward. Then, knowing what lies ahead for you, you won't become bored with being a Christian nor become spiritually dull and indifferent, but you will be anxious to follow the example of those who receive all that God has promised them because of their strong faith and patience."

Paul and Peter, faithful followers of Jesus and early apostolic leaders of the Church, acknowledged their dependence on God's favor and godly character. "And let us not grow weary while doing good, for in due season we shall reap if we do not lose heart." [121] Peter expanded on that thought by requiring that any speaking or ministering be done with the abilities that God had supplied. [122]

Yet some would try to have it both ways: dependence on riches and dependence on God. Jesus used the term *mammon* as the personification of riches. He said, "No one can serve two masters; for either he will hate the one and love the other, or else he will be loyal to the one and despise the other. You cannot serve God and mammon." [123]

Mammon is any form of materialism. It is impossible for us to serve God and, at the same time, exalt materialism. Neither can we worship God and, at the same time, drugs or alcohol or sex or pornography or power or any other carnal desire. Riches are materialism, money, mammon. Riches, Jesus emphasized, do not really belong to us; instead, we are stewards with the responsibility to use riches prudently to the advantage of the Kingdom of God. That is why God has given us the power to get riches and wealth.

Wealth is created by obedience to God's Word, will, and way. This obedience starts with faithful stewardship of the resources God has entrusted to us. In fact, the measure of our spiritual growth is determined by our stewardship of people, things, gifts, private property, money and relationship skills. Jesus pointed out that the pattern for this growth is always from small to large, from natural to spiritual, from others' to your own. "He who is faithful in what is least is faithful also in much; and he who is unjust in what is least is unjust also in much. Therefore if you have not been faithful in the unrighteous mammon, who will commit to your trust the true riches? And if you have not been faithful in what is another man's, who will give you what is your own?" [124] As this verse demonstrates, faithfulness in small things is not only vital it precedes lasting increase. [125] Wealth is the fruit of excellence in our lives. [126] Once we understand the difference between riches and wealth, we need to examine the stewardship responsibility.

## Stewardship responsibility

Basically, there are four aspects of our responsibility. First, we should tend and use our gifts as good stewards, understanding that a steward is the manager of another's household or estate. The property is not ours, but like the servants in the story of the talents we have the responsibility of wisely investing and increasing our Lord's property. "As each one has received a gift, minister it to one another, as good stewards of the manifold grace of God. If anyone speaks, let him speak as the oracles of God. If anyone ministers, let him do it as with the ability which God supplies, that in all things God may be glorified through Jesus Christ, to whom belong the glory and the dominion forever and ever. Amen." [127]

Second, we should allow God to teach us how to profit and lead us in the way we should go. "Thus says the Lord, your Redeemer, The Holy One of Israel: 'I am the Lord your God, who teaches you to profit, who leads you by the way you should go." [128]

Third, we should become purveyors of wealth in the kingdom. "And you shall remember the Lord your God, for it is He who gives you power to get wealth, that He may establish His covenant which He swore to your fathers, as it is this day." [129]

Fourth, we should always do things God's way. His way is for us to establish His covenant in the earth, which speaks of establishing His kingdom. If we do these things, we are beginning to follow God's pattern for our destiny.

## God's pattern for our destiny

God's pattern is *Promise, Problem, Provision.* First, there is God's promise of our destiny, followed shortly by problems. Obedience to His Word, however, develops godly character— our wealth—that allows us to solve our problems and results in riches coming to us for the advancement of the kingdom. Therefore, the pattern of Promise, Problem, Provision looks like this:

- There is always a problem between the promise of God and the provision of God.

- The problem brings out the character attributes of God.

- In solving the problem we must manifest God's attributes: faith, belief, honor, integrity, virtue, spiritual knowledge, patience, perseverance, wisdom, and favor.

- Power comes through incremental problem solving.

- Destiny comes through incremental problem solving. God's destiny is to expand His kingdom through His family. He has called us to build character, skills, and relationships that will survive death and leave a legacy to others. While riches will not survive death, the wealth of character will. Our goals, then, must be to imitate the goals, aspirations and purposes of our Creator. God entrusts us with caring for natural things before spiritual things. God gives us care over greater things based on our care of smaller things. Wealth is the product of stewardship over the gifts God has given us. Riches are material goods gained with or without obedience to God; i.e., unrighteous mammon is acquired by exploitation, crime, or purely worldly and carnal motivation. Wealth, which includes skills, spiritual knowledge, and character, is developed by obedience to God's laws and way of doing things.

The key to our future is found in our past. Moses is an excellent example of this principle. No one was better qualified to lead the children of Israel out of the bondage of Egypt. He grew up in Pharaoh's court and fully understood the protocol, mannerisms, and customs of the imperial ruler. He knew how to get things done and who would do them. He also lived in the Midian desert for forty years, which fully prepared him for the hardships of the wilderness. Moses had complete knowledge of the geography of the Sinai Peninsula, and he must have known that the cloud by day was leading them to a place where the army of Pharaoh would have Israel trapped. He knew God would deliver them. Likewise, the experiences of our past have prepared us for the future. Most of the problems we face are lessons to be learned, and most of our trials are to prepare us for future events.

Paul wrote about this testing in 1Corinthians 3:8–17, "The one who plants and the one who waters work as a team with the same purpose. Yet they will be rewarded individually, according to their own hard work. We work together as partners who belong to God. You are God's building—not ours.

"Because of God's special favor to me, I have laid the foundation like an expert builder. Now others are building on it. But whoever is building on this foundation must be very careful. For no one can lay any other foundation than the one we already have—Jesus Christ. Now anyone who builds on that foundation may use gold, silver, jewels, wood, hay, or straw. But there is going to come a time of testing at the judgment day to see what kind of work each builder has done. Everyone's work will be put through the fire to see whether or not it keeps its value. If the work survives the fire, that builder will receive a reward. But if the work is burned up, the builder will suffer great loss. The builders themselves will be saved, but like someone escaping through a wall of flames.

"Don't you realize that all of you together are the temple of God and that the Spirit of God lives in you?" (NLT).[130]

If, then, we make God's treasure our focus and concentrate on developing our talents for His glory, we are putting ourselves in position to establish dominion. Most of our trials and problems are lessons to prepare us for some future event, and any adversities will simply reveal the wealth of character. In the next chapter, we will take an in-depth look at how God uses patterns.

## Summary

- God created us for His glory, and He wants us to cover the earth with His will.

- God commissioned us and created us to conquer, for dominion.

- The *ekklesia*, the church, is the vehicle God uses to establish kingdom dominion.

- The church and the kingdom are not synonymous terms.

- The Holy Spirit anointing is present in each believer with power to minister.

- There is a ministry of business just as there is a ministry of preaching.

- All work is ministry.

- Problems are allowed by God to prove our faith and to develop our character.

- Adversity does not make the man; it merely reveals the man for what he really is.

- Wealth and riches are not synonymous.

- Riches are temporal. Wealth is eternal.

- Riches will not pass through death; wealth will.

- Riches are something we have; wealth is something we are.

- God will give riches to those who know how to create wealth.

- Riches do not lead to wealth, but wealth will lead to riches.

- Wealth is created by obedience to God's Word, His will, and His way.

- *Promise, Problem, Provision* is the pattern that leads to the next level of living.

- Most problems are lessons to be learned.

- Problems are allowed by God to prepare us for a future event.

- Christlike character is your destiny.

# • CHAPTER FIVE •

## GOD WORKS THROUGH PATTERNS

The Old Testament delineates the pattern God has established for the structure of government. This pattern begins with God giving the dominion commission of Genesis 1:26-28 in which he instructs man to be fruitful and to multiply, to replenish the earth, and to establish dominion over it. Then in the New Testament, Jesus calls His Church the *ekklesia,* the called out ones, the elected ones, and commands that we seek God's kingdom first. [131] In the last chapter, we learned that *ekklesia,* in Hellenistic societies, referred to a representative assembly that ruled in civic affairs; this group had influence over morals, values and ethical standards. Rome, of course, knew the real power of the traditional *ekklesia* and considered the newly formed *Ekklesia,* a threat. She recognized that the Church was not some weak, cowering, persecuted religious authority, but rather a real power. Terrified that the new organization might take over its world, Rome stepped up persecutions against the Church.

The question became, and still is today, Who is ruling our communities? Who determines the traditions and values of our communities? Who sets the moral tone and establishes ethical standards in our marketplaces, schools and governmental circles? Who has more influence in the lives of our children? Movies, musicians, entertainers or the *Ekklesia?* Hollywood, Madison Avenue, Wall Street, or the *Ekklesia?*

Although God wants to establish dominion through His kingdom, it has not been established because the Church is trying to do things "our way" instead of God's way. Our way seems to be to leave the responsibility for dominion up to the priests while the kings expend their energy and skills on amassing material goods for themselves. Even though it has been demonstrated that the kings are responsible for establishing dominion, they do not step forward and fulfill their responsibility. The kings simply are not doing their job, which is to put the Church in the position to influence the other spheres of government. As Dennis Peacocke relates, these five spheres are: self-government, family government, economic/commercial government, civil government and church government. It is God's plan that the Church influences the other spheres so His kingdom can be established. The Church is the vehicle that God uses to establish His kingdom. While the priests cannot influence the economic/commercial and civil spheres as effectively as can the kings, they do effectively influence self-government and family governments. Only the economic/commercial and the civil spheres are not effectively influenced by the Church. This is primarily because kings have not been taught that this is their role. Consequently, they have felt unappreciated, unnecessary and unneeded in the establishment of the kingdom. The priests know their roles fairly well, but the kings are just now beginning to understand theirs.

## God established two primary offices of government: kings and priests

Most of what I have learned regarding the offices of kings and priests I learned from the book, *Kings and Priests,* by David High. He teaches that when God established the two primary offices of government, kings and priests, He assigned specific roles to each. The role of the priests is to attend to God's glory. They hear from God and get the vision for the people. They offer sacrifices for sin, peace, and thanksgiving. They receive tithes and offerings, from which they maintain the house of God and care for widows, orphans, and the stranger at the gate. They speak encouragement to the army before battle. None of these duties bespeaks of dominion; they speak of guidance, forgiveness, providence, encouragement, and God's glory.

Dominion is the role of the kings. They destroy the enemies of God. They take the spoils and plunder of war. They pay tithes and offerings to the priests. They govern the physical affairs of the nation. All of these duties are necessary to establish a place for God's kingdom, to establish dominance over the earth.

Always, the roles were clearly defined. Priests advised the kings but never tried *to be* kings. Kings, at times, would give directly to the needs of the people but they were not permitted to cross the line and perform priestly functions. When they tried, they suffered the judgment of God. Witness King Saul who felt he had the right to bless Israel before going into battle. "And Samuel said, 'What have you done?' And Saul said, 'When I saw that the people were scattered from me, and that you did not come within the days appointed, and that the Philistines gathered together at Michmash, then I said, 'The Philistines will now come down on me at Gilgal, and I have not made supplication to the Lord.' Therefore I felt compelled, and offered a burnt offering.' And Samuel said to Saul, 'You have done foolishly. You have not kept the commandment of the Lord your God, which He commanded you. For now the Lord would have established your kingdom over Israel forever. But now your kingdom shall not continue. The Lord has sought for Himself a man after His own heart, and the Lord has commanded him to be commander over His people, because you have not kept what the Lord commanded you." [132]

## Examples of the biblical pattern

Only the priests were commanded to bless the king before going to war. "When you go out to battle against your enemies, and see horses and chariots and people more numerous than you, do not be afraid of them; for the Lord your God is with you, who brought you up from the land of Egypt. So it shall be, when you are on the verge of battle, that the priest shall approach and speak to the people. And he shall say to them, 'Hear, O Israel: Today you are on the verge of battle with your enemies. Do not let your heart faint, do not be afraid, and do not tremble or be terrified because of them; for the Lord your God is He who goes with you, to fight for you against your enemies, to save you.'" [133]

Divine teamwork between the priest and king was borne out of mutual respect and common interest, but God uses priests to remind us of our purpose, our vision and mission. [134] An example of this comes from the life of King David. During his reign, Israel was at war with Ammon, and the priest spoke blessings to the venture. "It happened in the spring of the year, at the time when kings go out to battle, that David sent Joab and his servants with him, and all Israel; and they destroyed the people of Ammon and besieged Rabbah. But David remained at Jerusalem." [135] It seems, however, that David lost his vision and planned for his personal pleasures instead of leading his people to war; this loss of vision led to sin. His seduction of Bathsheba led to betrayal and murder. Later he repented and returned to his original mission when Nathan, the prophet, confronted him with his sin.

Kings and priests never attempted to remove the other from his office lest they incur the wrath of God. Mutual respect was maintained, even if one was wicked. It was acknowledged that God selected the leaders, and only God could reject them. The Old Testament is replete with stories of kings and priests who sinned or were evil and other priests and kings who worked alongside, all the while warning them to repent. This is not to say that God was pleased with their sin; it merely emphasizes that God establishes and removes leadership.

The New Testament also emphasizes divine teamwork between kings and priests. Twice in the Revelation, John points out that God has made us kings and priests to God, to reign on the earth. "To Him who loved us and washed us from our sins in His own blood, and has made us kings and priests to His God and Father, to Him be glory and dominion forever and ever. Amen." [136] And again in Revelation 5:10, "And have made us kings and priests to our God; and we shall reign on the earth." The Church has gotten a fairly good grasp of the glory of God, but I don't think she fully understands the dominion of God. In the Old Testament, the priests handled the glory of God, but the kings established dominion; I believe God wants to continue that Old Testament pattern in the Church. As previously discussed, each of us lives his life on two levels, public vs. private. In private, we are both a king and a priest. As a priest, we pray with our wives, study the Bible with our children, and bless our family. As a king, we go to work and bring in the material needs for our family; we become the provider for the family. In public, however, each has a dominant anointing to be either a king or a priest.

Kings and priests are equally important for the kingdom. Anointing is required to plan and implement both a missions trip and a business plan. The same anointing is required for both spiritual and material missions, yet for a common purpose: that of advancing the kingdom of God. While God has ordained that the Church be a kingdom of kings and priests, we have made the Church a kingdom of priests by insisting that all who would serve God must be a priest. A quick look at the Old Testament, however, shatters this concept. Of the twelve tribes in Israel, only one was to be a tribe of priests. This tribe, Levi, was the smallest of the tribes.

The other tribes were warriors, conquerors, soldiers, protectors; they were kings who would establish dominion for Israel.

In the Church, however, we have not seen the kings functioning properly. We are overdeveloped in the priesthood and underdeveloped in the kinghood. The primary reason that we are underdeveloped in kinghood is because of the misconception that to be pleasing to God one must have a pulpit ministry. That idea leaves the rest of us wondering, *Why didn't God love me enough to call me into the full-time ministry? What did I do wrong?* So we imbibe the misconception that we are somehow second-rate believers. Because we are business people and do not have a pulpit ministry, we feel we do not quite qualify. Consequently, we do not perceive ourselves as valuable, vital or necessary for the fulfillment of God's plan on earth. We feel like spiritual failures because we have to work in the material realm and be involved in the tedious and disagreeable things of life. Little do we realize that work is a holy and sacred calling. Work preceded the Fall, and Adam worked in the garden every day. Therefore, work is holy unto God. The calling from God to be a king is absolutely essential to establishing the kingdom of God in the nation, and teamwork is vital to creating powerful, dynamic churches and to effectively impact the nation. The priesthood alone cannot impact the world and establish the kingdom of God. It takes teamwork. Kings and priests should respect each other more, and kings should be free to work in their gifting for the glory of God. Only then will kings be fulfilled.

## Kings fulfilled

Kings thrive on conquest; they are the conquerors. Their primary responsibility is to take dominion. In the Old Testament, they would go to war against the enemies of God, vanquish them and bring back the spoils and plunder to the priests so that the vision of God could be fulfilled for the nation. They are anointed to conquer, but the priests are commanded to bless them before they go into battle so that there will be provision to fulfill the vision of the priests. Without the blessing of God, the kings are not going to be successful in battle; and only in their success does God receive glory. The blessing of God also gives kings reason for going to war, and when they have reasons, their attitudes change. How the kings live daily, Monday through Friday, is as vital to the health of the kingdom as Sunday worship.

Kings understand that today's battlefield is the marketplace and that the wealth of the wicked is stored up for the just. These riches are not in the Church; they are in the world. It is the kings' responsibility to move that money out of the world into the Church. Do you think some major corporation is going to have a meeting of the board and vote to give the Church $5 billion next year? Nothing is impossible with God, but do not bet on it. Besides, that is not God's pattern. His pattern is to anoint men and women, His kings, to go out into the marketplace with courage, with favor, with wisdom, with creative strategies and new ideas to vanquish the enemies of God and bring back the spoils of war to the Church so the kingdom of God can be established and expanded throughout the nations and the world. That is God's pattern. It takes teamwork, both kings and priests.

Without the blessings of God, there is no success. If you are a business person like I am, each day when you awaken and your feet hit the floor, you had better start running and looking to the left, to the right, behind you and all around because there are people out there who do not play the game by the same rules as we play. It is for this reason that we need the blessings of God. That is why it is important to link up with a man of God to walk in lockstep and harmony with you. He will be blessing and speaking the Word of God over you so that you are successful in battle; and you, in turn, will bring provision to him to fulfill the vision of the kingdom of God. That is God's plan for the Church. That is God's plan for kings: to carry out great exploits for God.

In order to carry out these great exploits, kings must maintain eternal focus. Because man was created an eternal being, only eternal works bring him lasting fulfillment. No king is victorious because of his talent, or his intelligence, or his looks, but because of the anointing and favor of God. Those victories are not for our own consumption but for the sake of the kingdom. They will come no other way; God has no other plan. When we kings wake up and realize that establishing dominion is just as important as the glory of God, we will work together and be aggressive in the marketplace. God does not mind our having a nice lifestyle; but if we do not have a strong mission from God, our desire to conquer will spin off into selfish living. If we do not realize that our calling in life is ministry, that our anointing is to bring in provision for the vision, we will bring in general provision but we will waste it on ourselves. If we do not have a clear vision of our purpose in life, and if we do not have continuing revelation of God's will, we will have no discipline. We will become unruly, unrighteous, and fail to fulfill God's mandated mission. *The Living Bible* says we run wild. [137] The Spanish translation reads, we become like a wild, untamed horse. [138] Our focus is lost.

Need for conquest goes to other areas when focus is lost. A sure sign that focus is lost and the need for conquest has gone awry is when the king gets involved in sex outside of marriage, or pornography, or drugs and alcohol, or expensive toys, hobbies, and an overemphasis on sports. A king without a mission will search for other outlets to satisfy that need for conquest. When he finds that outlet, his prosperity will destroy him.[139] Whatever idol he establishes will destroy him. Overemphasis on power/money starts a downward spiral that leads to poor health, ulcers, insomnia, drug and alcohol dependence, broken families, poverty and eventually death. David wrote, "The fool has said in his heart, 'There is no God.' They are corrupt, and have done abominable iniquity; there is none who does good."[140] When a man loses the riches he covets and worships, his miseries have come upon him.

James examined this phenomenon and concluded that a man loses his riches because he does not have the character and maturity to manage them properly. "Come now, you rich, weep and howl for your miseries that are coming upon you! Your riches are corrupted, and your garments are moth-eaten. Your gold and silver are corroded, and their corrosion will be a witness against you and will eat your flesh like fire. You have heaped up treasure in the last days."[141] When we are focused on the kingdom, there is no need to look for excitement and fulfillment elsewhere, because nothing is more exciting than tying into a vision for God. Our lives are filled with God-ordained challenges, which leave less time for idolatry and misplaced priority. Priests generate vision faster than they can generate provision. That is because they are the eyes and heart of God; they hear His direction and timing before others do. They see a great harvest coming and are ready to prepare for it. They are ready to build buildings, hire staff, print training materials, develop youth camps and children's ministries and establish homes for orphans or the elderly. Yet, vision usually requires money, which is the responsibility of kings.

Vision is underdeveloped in kings and overdeveloped in priests. Priests become frustrated because they do not have the finances to fund the vision. This situation catapults them into talking more about the missing provision than about the existing vision. So they get out of their anointing by trying to raise the money themselves. In the meantime, the kings who are anointed by God to make money do not feel vital, necessary, or needed. They feel unappreciated and think they are second-rate believers. If they do come to church, the pastor locks onto them and wants to send them to Bible school or make pastors out of them. The kings protest, "I'm not anointed to be a preacher; I only know how to make a couple of million dollars a year." So they feel guilty and begin to withdraw from church because they cannot see the kingdom too. They see only a frustrated version of the priest's vision, the version about missing provision and the fundraisers. The church is full of frustrated kings listening to frustrated priests. Instead of dwelling on the frustrations, kings and priests need to focus on 1 John 2:20, 27, "But you have an anointing from the Holy One, and you know all things.... But the anointing which you have received from Him abides in you, and you do not need that anyone teach you; but as the same anointing teaches you concerning all things, and is true, and is not a lie, and just as it has taught you, you will abide in Him." [142]

Sadly, we have always thought that only spiritual leaders had the anointing, or we kings felt the anointing when we walked into the church but if fell off when we left. The Bible says the anointing abides *in* us so that we can do our jobs better, whether those jobs pertain to the callings of the priest or the kings. In fact, the first people who were anointed by the Holy Spirit were lay people. After God brought Israel out of Egypt, He wanted to build a Tabernacle, a dwelling place for His spirit among the people. Unfortunately, there were no skilled craftsmen among the Israelites; they had spent 430 years making bricks! God covered this situation with the anointing. "And the Lord said to Moses, See, I have called by name Bezelel, son of Uri, son of Hur, of the tribe of Judah. And I have filled him with the Spirit of God, in wisdom and ability, in understanding and intelligence, and in knowledge, and in all kinds of craftsmanship, to devise skillful works, to work in gold and silver, and in bronze, and in cutting of stones for setting, and in carving of wood, to work in all kinds of craftsmanship. And behold, I have appointed with him Aholiab, son of Ahisamach, of the tribe of Dan; and to all who are wisehearted I have given wisdom and ability to make all that I have commanded you." [143] Likewise, when we go into the marketplace to do battle for God, the anointing resides within us to enable us to succeed; we have wisdom, knowledge, understanding and good judgment, all the skills we need to excel.

When Samuel anointed David, was David a priest or a king? He was a king. Did he live a life that was pleasing to God? The Bible says God called David "a man after my own heart because he does my will." As a youth, he had been chosen by God to be king over Israel and Samuel had anointed him. The anointing oil on David's head symbolized three things: the presence of God, the power of God, the purpose of God. Wherever there is the presence of God, there is the power of God to fulfill the purpose of God. David's purpose was that he be king of Israel. Our purpose is that we be kings; the Holy Spirit anoints us with the presence of God to fulfill the purpose of God. God has anointed us to be kings to bring in provision to fulfill the vision of God for the nation. When we realize our value and our worth in the kingdom, then the kingdom of God will be established in our cities, our nation and around the world. It is God's plan for us to go into the marketplace with favor, wisdom, new ideas, and creative strategies to establish dominion. In order to do this, we must develop our kingship.

## Develop your kingship

The first step in developing our kingship is to avoid every thing that would divert us from God and religion. Riches, honors, and pleasures are three great hindrances of godliness, especially to those in high stations. John called these hindrances the "lust of the flesh, the lust of the eyes, and the pride of life." [144] Confronted by the rulers of the surrounding nations who had no idea of godly leadership, kings were particularly subject to temptations to live selfishly. Therefore, God established certain rules, outlined in Deuteronomy 17, for their guidance and protection.

A king must not gratify the love of honor by multiplying horses. [145] Not unlike our prestigious automobiles of today, the horse was a symbol of power and greatness. The man who rode a horse in a country where the common transportation consisted of walking or using asses or mules was considered very important. Therefore, though he might have horses for his saddle or his chariots, he should not place his servants on horseback. [146] Neither should he have many horses for his officers and guards, nor multiply horses for war lest he trust in them too much. [147, 148] During the days when Jehovah was king, His representatives, the judges, rode on asses. The reason for not multiplying horses was that this would create a tie with Egypt from which the Israelites had been delivered from slavery. The horses were brought by dealers out of Egypt and resold at a profit to the countries surrounding Israel. God did not want the people, especially the kings, to be infected with the idolatries of Egypt to which they were very prone. [149] Likewise, we should take heed of any honors, business practices, or conversations that could draw us back into sin.

A king must not gratify the love of pleasure by multiplying wives[150] To his undoing, Solomon became attracted to women, focusing on acquiring wives and concubines to the detriment of the affairs of the kingdom.

Under the guises of forming alliances to protect Israel, he brought into his home and the nation, women from many nations and indulged their whims, even to establishing altars to false gods and joining his wives in worshipping them.[151] Even Solomon in all his wisdom failed to see that there is no greater enemy than the indulgence of the flesh.

A king must not gratify the love of riches by greatly multiplying silver and gold.[152] While he is allowed a generous treasure, he must not oppress his people in order to multiply his money;[153] nor is he to deceive himself by trusting his riches or setting his heart upon them.[154] Finally, a king must not increase riches to be used upon himself selfishly. David greatly multiplied silver and gold while he was king, but it was never to be used on himself nor for his family; it was always to be used in the service of God.[155, 156]

The second step in developing our kingship is to apply ourselves to the law of God and make it our rule in everything. God's law must be to us better than all riches, honors, and pleasures; it must be to us better than many high-powered automobiles or many wives or millions in gold and silver. Here are the instructions God gave Israel: "Also it shall be, when he sits on the throne of his kingdom, that he shall write for himself a copy of this law in a book, from the one before the priests, the Levites. And it shall be with him, and he shall read it all the days of his life, that he may learn to fear the Lord his God and be careful to observe all the words of this law and these statutes, that his heart may not be lifted above his brethren, that he may not turn aside from the commandment to the right hand or to the left, and that he may prolong his days in his kingdom, he and his children in the midst of Israel."

If we follow this logic through, we see that God recognizes that the king and his family set the example for the nation. I believe that part of the emphasis on the king making a copy of the law lies in enforcing its law on his heart. There are five steps proscribed for this activity: (1) the king must write himself a copy of the law out of the original, which was in the custody of the priest who attended the sanctuary. (2) The king must have a new and fresh copy of the law. He could not use the worn-out copies handed down by his ancestors. (3) The king must copy the law himself; he could not have someone else copy it for him. He might have had servants and attendants who were better typists and writers, but they could not make the king's copy. Perhaps this insistence that the king copy the law himself showed honor for the law and taught him that no element of worship was beneath him. Most importantly, by writing the law himself, he was forced to know every detail of it and imprint it upon his heart and mind. (4) The king must make the copy, even though he was busy with the affairs of government. Obviously, the duties of a king require a large share of one's time and thoughts, yet the king was not allowed to put aside his attention to God's Word. Likewise, neither can we who are called to be kings in the marketplace let the busyness of our days excuse us from making God's Word and His vision first place in our lives. [157] (5) A king must read the law all the days of his life. Having written the law, the king could not consign his book to a cabinet to lie unread, but he must read it all the days of his life. It is not enough to have the Word of God, we must use it daily for guidance, nourishment and for strength. We must read it, we must consume it and apply it. The person who meditates on God's Word day and night prospers in all he does. [158]

The third step in developing our kingship is to apply the law to our life and business. The law of God must possess a king with a holy reverence to His divine majesty and authority. He must learn to fear God and to remember that no matter his status and stature in life, God is above him. The king must also observe the law continually and conscientiously obey it, both as a servant of God and as a good example to others. The king must exercise the virtue of humility and avoid all self-promotion. God's Word is to be a lamp to his feet and a light to his path — showing him where to go, what to do, what to say, and how to say it. Following God's law prolongs the days of our rule and prospers the lives of our families, friends and associates; for whoever honors God, is honored by God. [159] Following God's law also fills us with wisdom beyond our years and experience.

## Summary

- Priests handle the glory of God. Kings establish economic dominion.

- Kings, those in business, require the blessing of God to be successful in the marketplace (battlefield).

- Blessed and anointed businesspersons are used by God to transit the riches of the world into the church.

- When kings don't have a vision of who they are and their purpose, their anointing to conquer will spin off into unrighteous activities.

- Your talent can take you where your character cannot sustain you.

- The church is overdeveloped in priests and underdeveloped in kings.

- When kings are appreciated by priests, they will feel that their ministry is valuable, vital and necessary for the work of God in the earth.

- The anointing of the Holy Spirit symbolizes the *presence* of God, with the *power* of God to fulfill the *purpose* of God in the life of every believer.

- Kings must realize that they are blessed economically for the sake of the kingdom, not solely for their personal consumption.

- Kings must diligently study the Word of God for themselves. They must write out the Word of God and meditate therein to learn the wisdom and way of God for their lives and ministries.

- Kings should read Proverbs in the morning for wisdom and Psalms in the evening for courage.

- God will only honor those who honor Him.

- Character is destiny.

- Christlike character is your destiny.

# • Chapter Six •

## GETTING WISDOM

Pursuing this wisdom is the most important thing we can do, according to Proverbs 4:7, "Determination to be wise is the first step toward becoming wise: and with your wisdom, develop common sense and good judgment." [160] In the King James Version this verse reads, "Wisdom is the principal thing; therefore get wisdom: and with all thy getting get understanding." In contrast, the world promotes money as the principal thing and urges that we get more. In fact, this attitude has become the underlying attitude of our culture. But Solomon wrote, "How much better is wisdom than gold, and understanding than silver!" [161] He also questioned, "Why is there in the hand of a fool the purchase price of wisdom, since he has no heart for it?" [162]

Wisdom promises the seeker a number of things, among which are promotion and honor. "Exalt her, and she will promote you; she will bring you honor, when you embrace her. She will place on your head an ornament of grace; a crown of glory she will deliver to you." [163] She also brings long life, riches, peace, pleasure, and the totality of our lives. [164] One of the reasons she can make these promises is because of who she is. Wisdom is anointed common sense. Wisdom is the right use of knowledge, which is the acquiring of facts. Wisdom takes those facts, interprets them correctly and applies them to one's life. These aspects of wisdom imply the ability to use reason and shrewdness in the management of one's affairs. They also suggest a quickness of understanding and a penetrating insight and consideration preceding action on any project. Wisdom deals with the application of both business facts and the principles of God to one's life.

Three words are used in the Scriptures for wisdom: *sophia, phronesis,* and *sunesis.* "'While *sophia* is the insight into the true nature of things, *phronesis* is the ability to discern modes of action with a view to their results; while *sophia* is theoretical, *phronesis* is practical' (Lightfoot). *Sunesis,* understanding, intelligence, is the critical faculty; this and *phronesis* are particular applications of *sophia.*" [165] Wisdom is like an island; as it grows, its shoreline increases. The shoreline represents our awareness of how little we know; as we grow in wisdom, our knowledge increases along with the awareness of just how little we really know. None of us is complete in himself; all that we have and all that we are come from God. It is for that reason that God despises the proud and gives grace to the humble. It is through humility and the fear of the Lord that we acquire riches and honor and life. "The fear of the Lord is the beginning of wisdom, and the knowledge of the Holy One is understanding." [166]

We are to seek wisdom as for a buried treasure. Proverbs 4 urges us to pursue diligently wisdom, saying that she will preserve us and keep us. Acquiring wisdom requires work. Interestingly, in our search for wisdom, truth is revealed to us. Likewise, the knowledge of God does not come by explanation; it comes only through revelation. Though we are born of the will of God, [167] we can discover only what He reveals. In these days, God is bringing us back to the first church revelation. He desires the Church to know the manifold wisdom of God. [168] This wisdom is like the snowflakes: complex, multifaceted, and having many dimensions.

## Two types of wisdom

The Scriptures speak of two types of wisdom: worldly or human wisdom and godly wisdom. James describes both types: "Who is wise and understanding among you? Let him show by good conduct that his works are done in the meekness of wisdom. But if you have bitter envy and self-seeking in your hearts, do not boast and lie against the truth. This wisdom does not descend from above, but is earthly, sensual, and demonic. For where envy and self-seeking exist, confusion and every evil thing will be there. But the wisdom that is from above is first pure, then peaceable, gentle, willing to yield, full of mercy and good fruits, without partiality and without hypocrisy. Now the fruit of righteousness is sown in peace by those who make peace." [169]

The reason for the lack of wisdom is that there is no fear of the Lord. "The fear of the Lord is the beginning of wisdom: a good understanding have all they that do his commandments: his praise endureth for ever." [170] According to the Proverbs, "The fear of the Lord is to hate evil: pride, and arrogancy, and the evil way, and the froward mouth, do I hate." [171] Froward, *skolios,* means morally crooked and perverse. It has come forward in English to mean "habitually disposed to disobedience and opposition." Godly wisdom hates evil, pride, arrogance, and habitual disobedience and opposition. Is it possible that in our tolerant culture, we have lost some of the fear of the Lord?

## Lack of wisdom allows problems to invade

It is well known that problems come because of the lack of wisdom, the lack of fear of the Lord. "For you closed your eyes to the facts and did not choose to reverence and trust the Lord, and you turned your back on me, spurning my advice. That is why you must eat the bitter fruit of having your own way and experience the full terrors of the pathway you have chosen. For you turned away from me—to death; your own complacency will kill you. Fools! But all who listen to me shall live in peace and safety, unafraid." [172]

We desire easy solutions to these problems, forgetting that the scriptural pattern is to overcome through our faith. [173] Like Naaman, we want the man of God to pray over us and erase the afflictions. Naaman, commander of the Syrian army, had leprosy and a captive maiden shared with him that the God of Israel could heal him. So Naaman and his retinue made the arduous trip on horseback to Samaria, thinking the prophet would wave his hand over him and heal him. Instead of even receiving his distinguished presence, the prophet, Elisha, instructed his servant to tell the commander to go dip seven times in the Jordan River, a twisting, muddy river that rushed down an inclined plane broken by 27 rapids and precipitous falls. Immediately, Naaman thought about the Abana and Pharpar rivers in his homeland, clear streams that flowed across the plains and emptied into the three lakes of Damascus. He deemed these rivers far better for washing than the silt-filled, hazardous Jordan. It was obvious that Naaman had not learned the principle that humility precedes blessing. Yet not until after Naaman humbled himself and bowed to the wisdom of the prophet and obeyed, was he healed. The works of God are always predicated on faith; obedience to the Word of God is always by faith and that same obedience is evidence that we trust God. As long as we insist on our own way, the answer is delayed and the problem continues and seemingly becomes larger and more formidable until we submit to His wisdom. The problem enlarges until the blessing finally comes so that God receives the glory. Like Naaman, we desire victory over our problems, distresses and afflictions; we want a magical solution to our dilemmas, and we think that by our own virtue, our own righteousness, our own good works, or our own power of faith or spirituality or powers of intercession, we achieved the answer. Yet this attitude proves that we lack wisdom.

We lack wisdom because we lack the fear of the Lord. We indulge in fleshly activities to gratify our own lower nature, and we are trapped in our own human wisdom. We neglect prayer and meditation and then make prayerless and powerless decisions based on our personal preferences and presumption. Without consecrating our lives to God, we make decisions without godly counsel. We want the men of God to pray the prayer of faith, strike their hand over us and extricate us from our problems. We want victory without prayer, obedience or faith. We engage in magical thinking. We forget that God is a miracle worker, not a magician. He does not operate on a nickel and dime consecration; He will not give us a million-dollar blessing with a small-time consecration. Any man wanting a solution with no repentance and no deliverance to a new heart and mind toward God will never be satisfied, for God's strategy is to bring victory in our lives through wisdom. He commands that we seek for wisdom as for a buried treasure, to seek it wholeheartedly and to value it highly.

## Intertwined with the quest for wisdom is the virtue of humility

Pride indicates independence from God; humility demonstrates dependence upon God. Throughout the New Testament, this dependence on God is lifted up as desirable. Jesus said the one who humbled himself would be exalted.[174, 175] Peter wrote that we should be clothed with humility,[176] while James insists that God despises the proud and gives grace to the humble.[177] Even Satan lost his wisdom when he lost the fear of the Lord.[178] If we want wisdom, then we must pray for it and seek it, realizing that humility precedes wisdom. In our search, we must recognize and confess our own weaknesses and recognize that our level of wisdom will not surpass our level of humility. Even then we do not *discover* wisdom; God *reveals* it to us as we believe and act in humble faith.

If we lack wisdom, we are told to ask God for it. [179] Solomon prayed for wisdom and God exalted him. Humility always precedes wisdom. David humbled himself and sought forgiveness when confronted with his sin. Moses was the meekest man on the face of the earth and God used him to deliver a nation.

Humility was evidenced in the life of Jesus. He instructed all who would follow Him to "learn of me, for I am meek and lowly in heart." [180] He that humbles himself shall be exalted, according to Luke 18:14. [181] When speaking of His relationship with His Father, Jesus used the words *not* and *nothing* to indicate his humbled position: "The Son can do nothing of himself, but what he seeth the Father do." [182] Christ became nothing that the Father God might be all. [183] Even His teachings praise humility. "Whosoever therefore shall humble himself as this little child, the same is greatest in the kingdom of heaven." [184] The child trusts his parents to provide for and protect him; he has no worries at all. The child is teachable; he hungers for knowledge and truth. The child, whether he is a prince or a pauper, has no consciousness of social status. Humility places us in a position of dependence on God, which opens heaven's richest blessings to us. In the Beatitudes, Jesus taught that the poor in spirit would inherit the kingdom of heaven and the meek would inherit the earth. [185] Humility was also evidenced in the actions of Jesus. He washed the feet of His disciples and listened to children. He walked with common people, drank water from their wells, and shared their food. He walked when he could have ridden. He was free from arrogance because He knew that all He had came from God.

Lack of humility makes one guilty of the sin of pride. God actively opposes the proud because the lack of humility hinders faith, [186] which, along with obedience, is necessary to receive His promises. Humility before God is usually not the problem; we lack humility before our fellowman. This lack of humility causes us to have difficulty preferring one another. Over and over we are instructed how to treat others. "Love each other with brotherly affection and take delight in honoring each other.... When others are happy, be happy with them. If they are sad, share their sorrow. Work happily together. Don't try to act big. Don't try to get into the good graces of important people, but enjoy the company of ordinary folks. And don't think you know it all." [187] John asks, "If we do not love our brothers whom we see, how can we love God whom we cannot see?" [188] Evidence that we love God is manifested in our personal relationships, so is humility. Through humility, we become like Christ, we learn who we are, and we receive His love and give out of it. Through humility, we acknowledge what God has done, not what we have done. We clothe ourselves in humility when we serve one another and are humble before one another. And when we do these things, God lifts us up.

Humility is freedom from arrogance; this freedom grows out of the recognition that all we have and are comes from God. It allows us to think of ourselves no more highly than we ought to think. It requires us to feel that in God's sight, we have no merit and no right to prefer others to ourselves. Humility does not demand undue self-depreciation but rather encourages lowliness of self-estimation and freedom from vanity. It expresses a spirit of willingness and obedience and a lack of resistance to God's dealings with us. Humility must also be expressed towards those who wrong us, in order that their insults and wrongdoing might be used by God for our benefit. Humility is enjoined of God and is essential to discipleship under Christ.

Solomon, who was given the gift of wisdom, wrote in the Proverbs 22:4, "By humility and the fear of the Lord are riches and honor and life." Men desire three things most in their lives: riches, the honor and esteem of their fellow man, and a long life. Interestingly, all three are attained through humility and the fear of the Lord. Where the fear of the Lord is there will be humility. It is when we do not fear God that we become proud. Knowing this, Solomon observed in Proverbs 3:34 that, "God despises the proud and gives grace to the humble." Wisdom comes when we reverence and honor God, because the fear of God is the foundation and basis for all wisdom. It follows then that wisdom is the foundation and basis of a happy, successful and fulfilling life.

In speaking of wisdom, the Scriptures tell us that "Length of days is in her right hand, in her left hand riches and honor" (Proverbs 3:16 NKJV), and "Riches and honor are with me, enduring riches and righteousness" (Proverbs 8:18 NKJV). Knowing that wisdom is founded upon the fear of God, King David extolled, "Praise the Lord! Blessed is the man who 'fears the Lord,' who delights greatly in His commandments. His descendants will be mighty on earth; the generation of the upright will be blessed. Wealth and riches will be in his house, and his righteousness endures forever" (Psalm 112:1-4 NKJV).

And therein lies wisdom, the wisdom of the kingdom of God, the foundation of our hope.

## Summary

- Pursuing wisdom is the most important thing we can do in life.

- Wisdom brings promotion, honor, riches, and a long happy life.

- The Word of God is the wisdom of God. The more of the Word of God we possess, the more wisdom we acquire.

- Humility preceded wisdom.

- Humility precedes God's grace in our lives.

- Pray for God to give you wisdom to formulate a strategy that leads to victory.

- *Wisdom, Strategy, Victory, Glory* is the pattern for dominion in the earth. There is always glory in victory. Victory is born from a strategy that comes from the wisdom of God.

- Wisdom is anointed common sense.

- Wisdom is the application of truth.

- Wisdom is the right use of knowledge.

- Christlike character is your destiny.

# • CHAPTER SEVEN •

## WITHOUT HOPE, FAITH IS UNNECESSARY

**H**ope is the fuel that keeps the dream alive and pushes us toward action; faith is the certainty of *knowing* that catapults us into action. Faith is a common topic in many church groups. We talk about being saved by faith, being healed by faith, and living by faith. Yet we do not often mention *hope*. Having to do with the unseen and the future, hope, *elpis,* according to Vine's *Dictionary of New Testament Words,* is a "favorable and confident expectation." [189]

### Hope describes the happy anticipation of good.

As believers, our greatest anticipation is that of eternal life with Jesus Christ. Paul wrote that he had been sent to bring faith to those God had chosen and to teach them to know God's truth, the kind of truth that changes lives. His teaching was to give them hope of eternal life which God, who cannot lie, promised before time began. [190] Speaking of Jesus the Christian's hope, Peter said, "He indeed was foreordained before the foundation of the world, but was manifest in these last times for you who through Him believe in God, who raised Him from the dead and gave Him glory, so that your faith and hope are in God." [191]

### Hope describes the foundation upon which it is based.

Sometimes hope is based on things that are not from God. Acts 16 describes a slave girl possessed with the spirit of divination, who brought her masters much profit by fortune-telling. After she was delivered from the evil spirit and her masters saw that their hope of profit was gone, they dragged Paul and Silas before the magistrates.

By contrast, the believer's hopes are built on Christ. "To them God willed to make known what are the riches of the glory of this mystery among the Gentiles: which is Christ in you, the hope of glory." [192] Only hope that is built upon the surety of God and His kingdom never wavers.

## Hope describes the object upon which it is fixed.

Like the ground upon which hope is built, the object of our hope is vital. Paul demonstrates that the believer must have his hope solidly anchored in Christ Jesus. [193] When he does, he is well able to weather the storms of life that assail.

## Hope is a catalyst of faith.

"Faith is the substance of things hoped for, the evidence of things not seen." [194] When there is no hope of a better tomorrow, there is no need for faith. Without faith, it is impossible to please God, but faith cannot exist without a confident expectation of something good, which is the definition of hope; therefore, hope must be pleasing to God. Since hope is a requisite for faith and faith is a requisite for pleasing God, then the logical conclusion is that hope is necessary to please God as well. So get your hopes up! Many of us have been told for years, "Don't get your hopes up," but I believe God is saying to us, "Get your hopes up. Grasp the promises in my Word and confidently expect something good to happen in your life; hope for a better tomorrow."

The Apostle Paul called our Lord the "God of hope": "Now may the God of hope fill you with all joy and peace in believing, that you may abound in hope by the power of the Holy Spirit." [195]

John Calvin said, "Hope is the constancy of faith." Martin Luther said, "Everything that is done in the world is done by hope." In other words, every great accomplishment is done by hope. I believe that when we no longer hope, we no longer live. Hopes and dreams based on God's Word cause faith to spring up in our hearts to birth courage and perseverance, those character attributes that please God. When hope abounds, courage grows.

"But without faith it is impossible to please him: for he that cometh to God must believe that he is, and that he is a rewarder of them that diligently seek him." [196] Hope is the catalyst of faith; without hope, faith is unnecessary. Faith is a firm persuasion based on hearing God's Word and knowing His character that we are sure of His actions in any given situation. That is what the writer of Hebrews meant: we know God is and we know He rewards those of us who diligently seek Him. It is our hope that sparks the faith and enables it to fuel the vision, without which people perish. Without a vision, there is no restraint to do evil. Without a vision, there is no future. Without a vision, there are only our comfort zones.

## Summary

- Hope is the fuel that keeps the dream alive.

- Hope is the favorable and confident expectation of something good.

- Hope that pleases God is birthed from the promises of God.

- Hope is the catalyst of faith.

- Hope is necessary to please God.

- Hope is the constancy of faith.

- Every great accomplishment is done by hope.

- We worship the God of hope.

- Hope is the unfolding of our dreams.

- Without hope, we will never know what is beyond our vision.

- When hope abounds, courage grows.

- Without hope faith is unnecessary.

- Christlike character is your destiny.

# · CHAPTER EIGHT ·

## KICKING THE COMFORT ZONE

Too often we fail to look at the comfort zone versus growing in Christ. To grow we must get out of the comfort zone because it is more deadly than trials, tribulations or afflictions. In writing about the comfort zone, C. S. Lewis, the popular English writer, said, "The safest road to hell is the gradual one." Most of us have a tendency to grow only to the limit of the comfort zone. We are well aware that as long as we are in the zone, no special effort is required; no sacrifice demanded; no discipline encouraged; and no diligence extracted. There is nothing to do in the comfort zone, because nothing is happening there. Living in the comfort zone is easy; we know what to expect. But all growth occurs outside the zone.

As Dr. Gerald Brooks, pastor of Grace Outreach Center Plano, Texas, taught me, living is not growing. Just because we have put in the time does not mean we have grown. A man might say he has been a Christian for thirty-eight years, but that means nothing, because growing old in the Lord is not growing up. Growth is not automatic; it does not just happen. To grow, we must continually advance our learning of God's Word and His way, the closeness of our relationship with Him, and our walk with Him. The day we quit learning and advancing is the day we become obsolete.

We can get out of the comfort zone in two ways: (a) model someone, or (b) mentor someone. Depending on where we are spiritually, we may choose to model another businessman or a Christian leader. Modeling means that we propose that the individual we have chosen is worthy of imitation; we believe this individual's life aligns with God's Word and becomes a guideline for our own life. If our experience with God is relatively new or if we are not well-versed in the Scriptures, it may be that we will want to follow a model for awhile.

The second way to get out of the comfort zone is to mentor someone. In this case, we become the one who is followed. We set ourselves up as patterns for younger believers. Among those we mentor might be other men at the church, special interest groups, and children. When we start mentoring others, we will find that we will make greater demands on ourselves, demands that require more time spent in prayer, more study of the Word, and greater care given to our daily walk with Christ.

The primary mentoring responsibility of any parent is to our own children. When I became a Christian, I attended a seminar by Bill Gothard where I was instructed in the importance of meditating in God's Word and in teaching my children the Word of God. It was summertime and I would read a chapter in Proverbs every day to my two young sons. Additionally, I demanded that they memorize a verse of the Bible every day. So in the morning I would give them a verse to memorize, and in the evening they would recite to me, dutifully and faithfully, the memorized verse.

The Word of God is quick and powerful, and sharper than any two-edged sword, dividing between soul and spirit, joints and marrow. [197] The Word of God is Spirit and Life. As we memorize and meditate in the Word, it will dramatically change every area of our lives. When my children memorized the Word, it instilled discipline into their young lives. It expanded their minds and enhanced their ability to retain knowledge. My boys had always maintained good grades in school and they were always well behaved; however, after a summer of Bible memorization and devotion, their grades and behavior improved still more. Additionally, I enjoyed a level of intimacy with them that I had not experienced before. Plus, I established myself as a type of spiritual authority in my family that allowed me to exert discipline, leadership and humility that before had been difficult.

Dr. Edwin Louis Cole has taught me that prayer produces intimacy. When we pray, we become intimate "with whom you pray, to whom you pray, and for whom you pray." Praying with our children will produce a new level of intimacy and friendship, birthed in the spirit, that will enhance our relationship for the rest of their lives and into eternity.

I have had the privilege of not only being a father to my children but also being their friend and business associate. I have had the opportunity to have true fellowship with my sons by working with them in the ministry of our business. We have shared vision, responsibilities, mission, problems, and victories. We have learned together, lived together, and grown up together. We have lived in true fellowship with our children.

God chose to reveal himself to the world through Abraham, because. He saw in Abraham the character attribute of a man who would instruct his children in the Word of God. "For I have known him, in order that he may command his children and his household after him, that they keep the way of the Lord, to do righteousness and justice, that the Lord may bring to Abraham what He was spoken to him" (Genesis 18:19, NKJV). When God found a man He could trust to teach his progeny the Word of God, He knew Abraham would keep his covenant with Him. Then God could fulfill the promise He had ordained for Abraham's life. I believe that when we are faithful to teach our children the Word of God, we, like Abraham, qualify ourselves to have God's plan, promise, and potential fulfilled in our lives.

The reward of the trustworthy is more trust. When God knows He can trust us to be a faithful steward of our children by teaching them His Word, then He can trust us with more responsibility and fulfill His promise for our life.

So we need to get out of our comfort zone and mentor our children. In doing so, we will sow seeds that will reap an eternal harvest in every aspect of our life.

How comfortable are we where we are? If we are feeling comfortable at all, it is time to get out of the comfort zone and move to the next level. If we are not progressing, we are regressing. We do not stand still in our relationship with God or any place else in life. So go for it! Get out of that comfort zone!

## Strengths versus weaknesses

We all have both strengths and weaknesses. Since these strengths are gifts, there can be no pride of ownership; instead, we must recognize the gifts and define, refine and dedicate them to God. As good stewards, we are to use properly these gifts, seeking to blend these strengths with those of others. Thus, the kingdom is strengthened and we all have opportunity to grow.

However, some misunderstandings about strengths and weaknesses need to be considered. The first myth is that improving weaknesses will solve all your problems. Actually, focusing on a weakness with the hopes of improving it will produce, at best, an average skill. For example, many employers place employees in positions that have nothing to do with their strengths, expecting that the employee can make the new position his or her area of skill. It would be far more productive if the employer would recognize the strengths of his people and develop the best producers. The same is true with one's spouse, children, and business associates. Identify and invest in the best. Parents often focus too much on bad grades instead of encouraging the child to excel in the areas in which he makes good grades. The self-esteem that follows winning will enable the child to raise the bad grades somewhat, but probably never to the level of his areas of strength. In our own lives, we should focus on the things we do well and develop them, being careful not to allow ourselves to be drawn away in the areas of weakness.

The second myth is that strength will take care of itself. Sadly, we too often take our strengths for granted, tending to follow the old adage, "Be anything you want to be." Wrong! We can be anything our strengths allow us to be. I believe it is necessary for us to focus on our strengths; in fact, not to do so can only be regarded as sin. [198] Focusing on one's strength is the difference between being good at something and being great at something. If then we are not succeeding, we must check to see if we are building on a strength. This means that we must identify our strengths by asking these questions: What am I good at? What do others say I am good at? What do I enjoy? What is working? What do I have opportunities to do now? Where is the flow? As we are exploring these questions, we should watch for subjects of rapid learning, for glimpses of excellence, and places of anointing. The process is to identify, develop, refine, and dedicate. If we have multiple strengths, we should choose one and concentrate on it. Then find a mission for the strength—a goal, a purpose, a reason for existence. Focusing on multiple strengths leads to instability and lack of focus. For example, Luiciano Pavarotti had two strengths: teaching gymnastics and singing. What if he had tried to do both? Do you suppose he would have become the phenomenally successful tenor he is today? Finally, we manage our weaknesses by subcontracting them, by hiring someone else to do those tasks that would hinder our focusing on our strengths. Finally, our strengths show us God's plan for our lives. "A man's gift maketh room for him, and bringeth him before great men." [199] God thoroughly equips us to perform the good work He has outlined for us. [200] Therefore, as we focus on our strengths, our weaknesses become irrelevant.

## Anointing promotes you

The anointing of the Holy Spirit gives us *the edge*. By the edge, I mean the advantage, benefit, profitable favor that puts us over in life. If we do not have that anointing, we will be put under in life. Everyone in business is looking for the edge, not knowing that it comes through serving Christ. Sadly, many of us have forgotten we already have the edge. Jesus told the disciples, "It is expedient for you that I go away; for if I go not away, the Comforter will not come unto you; but if I depart, I will send him unto you." [201] With Jesus, the disciples always had the edge; it they had to pay taxes, they went fishing; if they were hungry, He gave them bread and fish. He was saying to them, "If you think you have it good now, wait until the Comforter comes." Jesus came to bring us the advantage in life. [202] The central issue is that to have this advantage, we must be led by the Spirit who reveals God's plan, purpose and promise. Charles Spurgeon, the English minister who pastored Metropolitan Tabernacle, said the enemy wants to keep us ignorant of this anointing. It is a fact that God has anointed us; therefore, the anointing abides in us. The question is, What are we doing with God's anointing? David's anointing by the Prophet Samuel symbolized God's presence, power, and purpose. The same symbolism follows our anointing.

In the workplace, the anointing of the Holy Spirit helps in four ways: it produces wisdom, favor, creativity, enhanced skills. For example, the Holy Spirit anointed Joseph, Jacob, and Peter in the creation of finances. Taxes were due for both Jesus and the disciples when Jesus sent Peter fishing to get the tax money. God gave Jacob a dream showing him how to increase his own flocks when his uncle was cheating him. Egypt was facing a serious famine and God showed Joseph how to start stockpiling food years ahead of time so that he could feed his country. In following God's instructions, although he did not know it, Joseph was also making provisions for his own family. Therefore, it is appropriate and biblical, I believe, that when we have financial needs to ask God to show us how to create wealth.

The Holy Spirit enhanced the skills of the men that were to build the Tabernacle. God's desire was to dwell with His people so He commissioned the Tabernacle. The catch was that none of the men He handpicked had any construction skills; in fact, Israel had spent more than four hundred years making bricks. So God chose Bezaleel and anointed his natural strengths and made of him an anointed craftsman. With the anointing, he had answers no one else could provide; he developed skills that no one expected, all for God's purposes.

Joseph believed the anointing brought God's intended purpose. From the dreams of his early childhood, to slavery, to second in command of Egypt, Joseph's life reads like supernatural guidance. Despite the hardships and trials he faced, Joseph was certain that his life was following God's intended purpose. So it should be with us, our first responsibility should not be to make money but to represent Christ. The anointing directs us according to God's wisdom, not the market trends. For this reason, we can enjoy what we do and know that our decisions will be sound.

The Holy Spirit also enables us to make good decisions. It is said that we make about 1 thousand decisions a day, 365 thousand a year; and in an eighty-year life, we make more than 29 million decisions. Out of all of those, about twelve decisions change the direction of our lives. That is why it is important to submit each one to the guidance of the Holy Spirit, for His wisdom and His timing.

## Summary

- Most of us live and worship in our comfort zone.

- Living in the comfort zone is easy because we know what to expect.

- Living in the comfort zone is dangerous because we do not grow.

- All growth occurs outside of the comfort zone.

- If we are comfortable where we are spiritually, GET OUT OF THE COMFORT ZONE!

- We get out of our comfort zone by modeling someone and mentoring someone.

- God has given us a strength, a talent, an ability; He has made us special.

- God wants us to focus on our strengths. The world wants us to focus on our weaknesses.

- If we focus on our weaknesses and strive to improve the weaknesses, all we will ever be is average.

- God did not make us to be average; He made us for excellence.

- When we focus on our strengths and improve the strengths, we have the opportunity to become excellent.

- God's plan for our life revolves around the strengths He has given us.

- Find a partner who is strong where you are weak.

- When we go to our strengths and focus on our strengths, our weaknesses become irrelevant.

- Jesus came to give us an advantage in life. He gives us the edge we need.

- The anointing of the Holy Spirit brings wisdom, ability, and knowledge into our lives to help us do our jobs better.

- Christlike character is your destiny.

# • CHAPTER NINE •

## PRINCIPLES OF CAREER ADVANCEMENT

God wants to bless, promote and reward us. In blessing us, He desires to empower us to increase. "But ye are a chosen generation, a royal priesthood, an holy nation, a peculiar people; that ye should shew forth the praises of him who hath called you out of darkness into marvelous light." [203] Taken from the Greek *eklektos,* chosen means "selected out of a larger group for special service or privilege." Another interesting word in this passage is peculiar, *peripoiesis,* which is correctly translated "God's own possession." Understanding then that we are handpicked and named God's own people, it is easy to believe that God has a destiny for each of us. He has a plan for our lives; He has designed us for a specific place in His kingdom; and He has given us the ability to fulfill it. With that in mind, look at the ongoing privileges and plans He has for us. He is thinking about us right now. [204]He wants to make us perfect. [205] He wants to give us a future and a hope. [206] We are His workmanship, created for good works. [207] He has blessed us with every spiritual blessing, after having chosen us and predestined us. [208] With this kind of heritage and future, how can we fail at anything we attempt?

### Two primary objectives

God's plan is not revealed to us all at once; it is revealed incrementally as we walk in obedience to His will. This plan has been designed meticulously; and it involves vision and principles. Without a vision, we perish. [209] With a vision, we know our goal, are not easily frustrated, are focused, changed, strengthened, and sustained, and we learn to discipline ourselves to live a holy life. To please God, we must act upon His principles. The Scriptures teach that God is continually searching for those who will obey Him: "For the eyes of the Lord run to and fro throughout the whole earth, to shew himself strong in the behalf of them whose heart is perfect toward him. Herein thou has done foolishly: therefore from henceforth thou shall have wars." [210] If we read this verse closely, we will notice that immediately following the promise of protection and blessing is a promise of destruction. This is true of virtually every promise God has given us; each is conditional upon our obedience. God never leaves us uninformed about the results of our actions. If we obey, we receive the good; if we do not, we receive the bad.

Acting upon His principles starts with faith and vision. Unless we have a vision, a hope, or a dream that God has something significantly better for us than where we presently are, then we cannot have faith that is pleasing to God. Belief is not faith until it is acted upon. The writer of Hebrews wrote of this in 13:21: "Make you *perfect* in every good work to do his will, working in you that which is well pleasing in his sight, through Jesus Christ; to whom be glory for ever and ever. Amen." Being perfect is not meant in the sense of being flawless or never making a mistake; rather it derives from *katartizo*, which means "continually changing, constantly adjusting, in a state of repair, being mended, begin restored to what you ought to be."

While obedience is our part, restoration is God's. Paul writes that God has blessed us, chosen us and predestined us according to His will. [211] We are His workmanship, *poiema*, created unto good works, *agathos*. *Poiema* means, "designed by a master creator, a grand artisan. Something meticulously made and designed for a specific purpose." *Agathos*, good works, means "excellence; attractiveness; of good constitution or nature; useful, producing benefits; good, pleasant, happy; distinguished; upright, honorable." The topic of believers producing good works is fairly common in Paul's writings. He told the Corinthians that God would make them "abound to every good work." [212] To the Philippians, he wrote, "Being confident of this very thing, that he which hath begun a good work in you will perform it until the day of Jesus Christ." [213] The Colossians were instructed to be "fruitful in every good work," [214] while Timothy was to be prepared and "thoroughly furnished unto all good works." [215, 216] Titus was urged to be zealous of and to maintain good works. [217] Peter told believers that unbelievers would be able to glorify God because of the believers' good works. [218] God's plan for us is for good and not for evil and He intends that we should reach the destination He has planned for us. For that reason, God orders our steps, [219] establishes our way, enables us to be strong, and to do great exploits. [220] Our part is always the same: to believe, obey and fear the Lord. [221] His destiny for every person is to reveal Christ to the world, to show forth the praise of God, [222] and to bring glory to God. [223]

## Patterns and Principles: Our path of obedience

The more we base our lives on kingdom principles and on building our characters, rather than our personalities, the straighter will be our course. All true happiness and success are born out of a Christ-like character, which is more important than talent or education, and is the cornerstone of faithfulness. Obedience to principles, on the other hand, is the key for unlocking God's will. All the principles in the Bible are kingdom principles, and all are eternal and absolute. Methods are temporary and may change, but principles remain through every age and under every circumstance.

That is why knowledge, understanding and wisdom are so important to destiny. As discussed earlier, knowledge is the acquiring of facts, understanding is the interpretation of those facts, and wisdom, the application. To walk in the wisdom of God is to apply His Word to our lives by becoming doers of the Word and not hearers only. We walk in the wisdom of God, we walk in the way of God, when we walk in the Word of God. This formula is integral to success: the word, will, way and wisdom of God. This, of course, necessitates knowing the Word of God and understanding it; but unless we apply it and live by it, we will not fulfill God's ultimate plan and purpose. I believe that when God created us He cut us, stamped us and formed us for a specific and significant purpose: to be witnesses for the love and service of Jesus Christ. This love is best demonstrated through obedience, by doing the next thing He tells us to do. As we walk in this kind of obedience, we not only fulfill but we discover God's plan and bring glory to Him. Each step of obedience leads to an ever-growing and ever-maturing likeness and character of Christ. [224]

Following the establishment of a relationship of obedience, one must develop stewardship and leadership. God has given us: (1) principles to live by; (2) promises to believe in; (3) examples to follow; and (4) commandments to obey. He wants us to have a life of significance, but, sadly, we live on one of three levels: survivor, success, or significance. On the survivor level, where most of us live, we just get by; we live paycheck to paycheck, we have no time for friends or family, and we are generally too stressed and too exhausted to enjoy life. About twenty-five percent of us live at the success level and, for most, it is a temporary visit, not a permanent position. At this level, we have abundance, comfort, and an independent lifestyle. Yet it becomes temporary because common sense seems to fly out the door, and we treat this abundance as though it was achieved through magic, not hard work, talent, and obedience to God. The most important level is that of significance; on this level, we give generously to God and to others, always conscious that we are channels through which God can work.

With this background on patterns and principles, we will now look at nine principles, which, if obeyed, will transform our lives and place us in that position of significance.

## Principles of Advancement
### Principle 1. Relationship to Fellowship

Relationship comes by birth, but fellowship is initiated by a deep-seated desire and commitment to grow in Christ and to practice the presence of God. Jesus said this another way: "But seek ye first the kingdom of God, and his righteousness; and all these things shall be added unto you." [225] Jesus said He had come that we might have life abundantly, *perissos,* "above the common." This tells me that God has no interest in our barely getting along. However, to receive this abundance, we must go beyond relationship to fellowship with Jesus. There is an important difference. We are related to our fathers by birth, but not all of us have fellowship with our fathers. That is because we do not work at getting to know them and being in their presence. If one is born again by the Spirit of God, he has a relationship with Jesus, but he may not be in fellowship. Relationship will get us to heaven, but fellowship allows us to fulfill God's purpose and please God.

How then does one enter into such a fellowship? Let us look at the characteristics of a person with a deep and intimate fellowship with God. First, it is important that we diligently seek and desire God's constant presence. Second, long-term faith overcomes short-term disappointments. That is why we seek Him. What we learn today, we will use tomorrow.

Likewise, what we should learn today, we will use tomorrow. If we approach God casually and conveniently, we will not grow. We are being prepared today for some event in the future; therefore, we must feed our spirits every day. The writer of Hebrews defined faith as "the substance of things hoped for, the evidence of things not seen." [226] I believe a simpler definition is: Faith that pleases God is faith that believes "that God is, and that He is a rewarder of those who diligently seek Him." [227] Vision gives birth to hope, the belief that God has something significantly better planned. Without hope, faith is unnecessary. Hope is the extension of faith; therefore, hope must be pleasing to God. The reward is the fulfillment of the hopes, dreams and visions that God has placed in our hearts. Perhaps it is time we got our hopes up. A lame man encountered Peter and John in front of the temple in Jerusalem. "And a certain man lame from his mother's womb was carried, whom they laid daily at the gate of the temple which is called Beautiful, to ask alms of them that entered into the temple; who seeing Peter and John about to go into the temple asked an alms. And Peter fastening his eyes upon him with John, said, Look on us. And he gave heed unto them, expecting to receive something of them." [228]

He was doing exactly what King David had told Israel to do centuries before: "Delight yourself also in the Lord, and He shall give you the desires of your heart." [229] Isaiah, the prophet, also urged delight in God, "'...then the Lord will be your delight, and I will see to it that *you ride high* and *get your full share of the blessings* I promised to Jacob, your father.' The Lord has spoken." [230]

If we look again at the threefold definition of faith: (1) believing that God is; (2) believing that God is a rewarder; (3) believing that God is a rewarder of them that diligently seek Him, we understand that it is the Father's good pleasure to give us the kingdom. [231, 232] Before He can do that, He must be able to trust us. He wants our character to be mature enough to live in the kingdom. If we are not mature, it would be like giving a million dollars to a child. He would not know what to do with it. Enoch, described in the book of Jude as "the seventh from Adam," had the testimony that he pleased God. All we know about his life is that after the birth of Methuselah, Enoch "walked with God three hundred years." While no one knows for sure, I believe this walking with God was an intimate fellowship, a conversational intimacy, with God, where Enoch and God talked with each other. What the Scriptures do tell us is that he so pleased Him that God simply translated him to heaven. "By faith Enoch was translated that he should not see death; and was not found, because God had translated him: for before his translation he had this testimony, that he pleased God." [233] Enoch diligently sought the Lord and had intimate fellowship with God; because of that, he received the ultimate promotion.

Likewise, He will promote us and set us on high above all nations. God does not mind our having rewards. In fact, He wants us to have them. To please Him we must believe that He is a rewarder. When we diligently seek Him, He will give us abilities that we do not now possess. The assurance of His reward is diligence, the steady application of effort. Diligence has nothing to do with speed, but steady constancy; the diligent man pursues his objective without stopping. Diligence will produce rewards; it is just a matter of time. That is why God desires us to spend time with Him in prayer, praise, meditation, and the study of His Word. To seek God diligently is to seek and desire His constant presence, to be one with Him in prayer and meditation, to practice His presence, to pray without ceasing, to be in continual communication with Him, to think His thoughts, feel His feelings, to say His words and work His works. Seeking the Lord puts us in the place to hear God. As we seek Him, we are more fully prepared to meet the day. God draws nigh to those who draw nigh to Him. As we practice His presence, we will know what to do because we will hear His still, small voice. [234] We will see with increasing clarity God's plan and purpose.

## Principle 2. Diligence brings rewards

God wants us to be diligent in every area of our lives. There is a singlemindedness to diligence, a ruthlessness, steadfastness, persistence and focus. Being diligent means setting our faces like flint and paying careful attention to all details. The following scriptures point out what is expected under diligence:

- Whatever your hand finds to do, do it with all your might. [235]

- Whatsoever ye do in word or deed, do all in the name of the Lord Jesus, giving thanks to God and the Father by him. [236]

- And whatsoever ye do, do it heartily, as to the Lord, and not unto men. [237]

- Do you see a man who is diligent in business? He shall stand before kings. [238]

- The hand of the diligent will bear rule. [239]

- The soul of diligent shall be made fat. [240]

- The thoughts of the diligent tend only to plenteousness. [241]

- And, finally, Moses, in writing the law, promised, "And it shall come to pass, *if ye shall hearken diligently unto my commandments*, which I command you this day, to love the Lord your God and to *serve him with all your heart and with all your soul*, that I will *give you the rain of your land in his due season*, the first rain and the latter rain, that thou mayest gather in thy corn, and thy wine, and thine oil, and I will send grass in thy fields for thy cattle *that thou mayest eat and be full.* [242]

## Principle 3. Meditation is the birthplace of creativity

To meditate is to focus one's thoughts on something so as to understand it deeply. Since it is the most effective way of knowing God, this focus begins with God's Word. God wants us to seek and desire His constant presence. Consider the following scriptures:

- Blessed is the man that walketh not in the counsel of the ungodly, nor standeth in the way of sinners, nor sitteth in the seat of the scornful. But his delight is in the law of the Lord; and in his law doth he meditate day and night. And he shall be like a tree planted by the rivers of water, that bringeth forth his fruit in his season; his leaf also shall not wither; and whatsoever he doeth shall prosper.[243]

- Think about these laws every day and every night so that you will be sure to obey all of them. For only then will you succeed. Then remind others about them. [244]

- Your word have I hidden in my heart, that I might not sin against You!. [245]

It is through meditation that we focus on our gifts: "Till I come, give attendance to reading, to exhortation, to doctrine. Neglect not the gift that is in thee, which was given thee by prophecy, with the laying on of the hands of the presbytery. Meditate upon these things; give thyself wholly to them; that thy profiting may appear to all." [246]

Prosperity is a by-product of a relationship with God. Some have said that prosperity is a heresy of the church; but rather than being a heresy, I believe, it is the natural, sequential, ordered result of righteousness. It is natural for a believer to prosper. Over and over the Scriptures state, "If you do these things, you will prosper." For example, if we raise our children in the nurture and admonition of the Lord and provoke them not to wrath, our relationship with them will prosper. If we love our wives as Christ loves the church, our marriages will prosper. If we esteem our fellow man as better than ourselves, our business and social relationships will prosper. If we are diligent in our business, we will stand before kings and not before obscure men; we will prosper. All of these things seem to be natural sequential results. That is because honest meditation on the Word of God prevents our making prosperity the goal and refocuses our thinking toward obeying God's commandments. As a result, whatever we do in righteousness will prosper.

Does God want us to prosper so that we can live in mansions and drive Rolls Royce automobiles? No! God wants us to prosper for the sake of the kingdom, so the Church can prosper, so the gospel will prosper, so people can be saved. Moses said it best in Deuteronomy: "And you shall remember the Lord your God, for it is He who gives you power to get wealth, *that He may establish His covenant* which He swore to your fathers, as it is this day."[247] God teaches us to prosper in order to establish His covenant; but the dire warning is that if we turn away from Him, we will perish. So it is incumbent upon us to focus on fellowship with God, not the by-products of that fellowship; God will Himself take care of those.

## Principle 4. Anointing

The central issue in our lives is the anointing of God. Each of us received the anointing at the moment we received Jesus as Savior and Lord; therefore, we are to live and walk with Him every day in every thing we do or say. We are to practice the presence of God. "But ye have an unction from the Holy One, and ye know all things . . . But the anointing which ye have received of him abideth in you, and ye need not that any man teach you: but as the same anointing teacheth you of all things, and is truth, and is no lie, and even as it hath taught you, ye shall abide in him."[248] We have an advantage in Christ. Because of the anointing, we have the mind of Christ and the gifts of the spirit available to us. We have these gifts when we negotiate contracts, hire employees, take employment, change jobs, for every action in every area of our lives.

Another way that we have the advantage is that we have the ability to communicate with God spirit to spirit. We are all aware of our five senses—sight, sound, smell, taste, and touch—and some of us realize there is a sixth sense which is a mental power, reason, that dominates the other five. Yet originally we were created, in Eden, with a seventh sense, the ability to communicate with God spirit to spirit. That ability is what the Scriptures refer to as the still small voice of guidance. Isaiah described it as "a word behind you, saying, 'This is the way, walk in it,' whenever you turn to the right hand or whenever you turn to the left."[249]

The ability to communicate with God spirit to spirit is not reserved only for those in ministry, but is available to every believer. The anointing of God reveals a believer's place and purpose in life. In fact, the *Amplified Bible* shows *anointing* to mean "sacred appointment." Most men do not live as though the anointing of God is on them; they simply are not aware of the presence of God in their daily lives. Satan would like to keep us in ignorance and in inferiority, not recognizing God's anointing and the significance of our lives. We need to understand three basic truths regarding the anointing: (1) the anointing of God is present within us; (2) the power of that anointing is in us; and (3) the purpose of the anointing.

God's anointing is more valuable than silver or gold. If a geologist told us a vein of gold was in our backyard, we would do everything in our power to mine the gold. Yet we have within us the anointing of the Holy Spirit which is far greater. The anointing is simply the ministry of the Holy Spirit in our life as He brings about the plan, purpose and the promise of God. It is not some mystical, mysterious force but is the power of God working on our behalf. In the Old Testament, the anointing was symbolized by the pouring of oil on the recipient's head. This anointing always revealed the purpose, power and presence of God. For example, the anointing of David by the prophet Samuel signified God's purpose for him to be king of Israel. The anointing of Samson empowered him to destroy the enemies of his people, and the anointing of the prophet Samuel signified God's presence with and communication through him. While only the prophets, priests and kings were anointed in Old Testament times, now God has anointed each believer. "Now he which stablished us with you in Christ, and hath anointed us, is God." [250] Unfortunately, we tend to limit the anointing to the supernatural manifestations that occur in church services and think only of the dynamics of the anointing. We have overlooked the practical aspects of the anointing. God wants to anoint both our finances and the creation of our finances. He also wants to anoint us in the workplace with favor, wisdom, creativity, enhanced skills, and the ability to make correct decisions.

## Principle 5. Decisions

Timing is the essential ingredient in success: being the right person, at the right place, at the right time. The average person makes over a thousand decisions every day; however, only twelve life-changing decisions have a direct impact on the direction of our lives. The problem arises in that we never know when those twelve decisions will manifest themselves. It is like in a football game. While there are approximately 120-130 plays in the average game, only five or six decide the outcome. So each play must have the same focus, the same diligent effort, and the same intensity. In the critical decisions of life, God has anointed us to know the correct decision to make.

Daniel is an example of this anointing for making decisions. "Inasmuch as an excellent spirit, knowledge, understanding, interpreting dreams, solving riddles, and explaining enigmas were found in this Daniel, whom the king named Belteshazzar, now let Daniel be called, and he will give the interpretation." [251] Again, in Daniel 11, we are told that people who know their God shall be strong and carry out great exploits. Among these exploits are workaday situations in which we need God's favor. For example, He gives us wisdom when we lack it, strength when we fail, creative ability to devise better methods and techniques. The anointing enhances our abilities and promotes us in business. He gives us wisdom for strategies, creativity for problem solving, favor with customers and employers, and enhances our skills to perform the necessary tasks. Our jobs are our ministry. Whether we are lawyers, doctors, mechanics, salesmen, managers, whatever we do, we need the anointing of the Holy Spirit to help us do a better job.

As men of God filled and led by the Holy Spirit, we should be able to find solutions to problems when others cannot find them. For example, Joseph was anointed to be a businessman in Egypt. His wisdom so impressed Potiphar and Pharaoh that he was continually promoted until he became second to Pharaoh. Despite the struggles of his early life, he showed his recognition of the supernatural anointing in the names of his sons: his firstborn was called Manasseh, *made to forget,* and the secondborn, Ephraim, *fruitfulness.* Isn't it an interesting corollary that before Joseph could enter into fruitfulness he had to forget the mistakes and errors of his past? He had to forget his being mistreated by his brothers, by Potiphar's wife, and his being forgotten in jail. He had to forgive so he could forget. He had to forget before he could enter into fruitfulness.

Jacob was anointed by God to be profitable as a shepherd. His Uncle Laban used treachery and subterfuge to keep him in his employ, but God taught him how to win in a seemingly no-win situation. Even Peter who fished all night and caught nothing was instructed by Jesus to throw his net in one more time; he caught so many fish that it was obvious to his fellow fishermen that a supernatural miracle had occurred. We, too, have the potential for seeing miracles happen in our business lives. All it takes is establishing fellowship with Jesus, cultivating it and walking in strict obedience to His commandments. As we walk humbly with Him, we bring honor to Him.

## Principle 6.  Honor God

Many of us are not experiencing God's best because we fail to honor Him. Sin, of course, dishonors God; but we dishonor Him also in other ways, mainly through actions caused by disobedience and lack of trust. The Scriptures consistently teach that obedience is better than sacrifice. You cannot gain by sacrifice what you lose through disobedience. The kingdom of God operates on a covenant exchange where we give God first place in our lives, recognizing Him as our source. Disobedience and mistrust invalidate the covenant. God keeps covenant and honors only those who honor Him, with their substance, obedience, trust, in all areas of life. Since the next chapter deals with this subject in greater detail, we will look now at the other principles of career advancement.

## Principle 7.  Forget and forgive the past.

Dr. Gerald Brooks of Grace Outreach Center in Plano, Texas, taught me much about forgetting and forgiving. He taught me that many of us are controlled and influenced by the past; we are shackled by past failures, mistakes, or poor judgment. That is why it is important to forget the past and forgive ourselves. "Forget the former things; do not dwell on the past. See, I am doing a new thing! Now it springs up; do you not perceive it? I am making a way in the desert and streams in the wasteland." [252] Forgetting is the pivotal point, the one that will make or break us. Too many of us are controlled by fear of failing again. We become like puppets that appear to be acting independently but who are, in reality, controlled by strings from the past. Often we do not take the risks necessary to succeed because of our fear of failure. The Apostle Paul, whose early life was filled with spiritual failure, wrote, "…one thing I do, *forgetting* those things which are behind and reaching forward to those things which are ahead, I press toward the goal for the prize of the upward call of God in Christ Jesus." [253]

Forgetting does not mean a failure will be erased from memory; it only means that the failure is defused and loses its power to hurt and paralyze us. A good way to know whether we have forgotten is to notice how much we dwell in the past: talking about it, reliving it, embracing it. We cannot more forward while we are embracing the past. Falling does not mean utter ruin. "For a righteous man may fall seven times and rise again." [254] All success is born out of failure. As previously mentioned, Edison accumulated ten thousand failures before he had a lead storage battery. American entrepreneurs average failing at business 3.2 times before they succeed. The hundred wealthiest men in our country averaged seven failures. When asked his secret of success, Benjamin Franklin said, "I'm not afraid to fail." The secret of success is that we fail our way to success, so we need to forget the past.

One reason we have difficulty forgetting is that we have not forgiven the source of the failure, whether that be others or ourselves. Jesus pointed out the necessity of forgiveness: "And when ye stand praying, forgive, if ye have aught against any: that your Father also which is in heaven may forgive you your trespasses." [255] The commandment here is to take important, painful things and make them unimportant through the process of forgiveness. True forgiveness releases the ability to forget. For example, in Jeremiah, God said, "I forgive them their sins and remember them no more"; and again in Hebrews, "I have forgiven your iniquities and I remember them no more." He forgets our past so He can love us in the future. If we are true believers committed to walking with Him, we will follow His example. Forgiveness is not about whether the other person was right or wrong, or whether the situation hurt, or whether we are giving permission for someone to hurt us again, or whether we condone another's actions. Forgiveness is about releasing ourselves and the other person from resentment, anger, and revenge. W. E. Vine says that in its verb form, forgive means "to send away"; and in its noun form, "to receive." When we forgive, we are sending away the emotional baggage so that we can receive healing from the hurt.

Corrie ten Boom illustrates this concept of forgiveness. The Ten Boom family of Haarlem, Holland, were devoted Christians who demonstrated their love for Christ by serving their fellow man. Their home, which was located above the family clock business, was always open to those in need. During the Second World War, that shelter became a refuge for those being hunted by the Nazis: Jews, students who refused to join the Nazis, and members of the Dutch underground resistance movement. Corrie, her father Caspar and her sister Betsie, risked their lives during 1943 and into 1944. Always six to seven people were hidden in the house and others stayed for a short time until other safe houses could be found for them. Through these activities, the Ten Boom family and their friends saved the lives of approximately 800 Jews and protected numerous Dutch underground members.

On February 28, 1944, the family was betrayed and the Gestapo raided the house and arrested the family and everyone who came to the house or shop. By the end of the day more than twenty people, including other family members had been arrested. Although the Gestapo systematically searched the house, they could not find the six people who were secreted behind the walls. Caspar, 84, was sent to Scheveningen Prison where he died after only ten days. A nephew, 24, was sent to Bergen Belsen and never returned. Corrie's brother, Willem, 60, a leader in the Dutch underground, contracted spinal tuberculosis in prison and died shortly after the war.

Corrie and Betsie were sent to three different prisons, and after ten months, wound up in the infamous Ravensbruck concentration camp near Berlin. Despite the unbearable conditions in the camp, Betsie and Corrie spent their time sharing Jesus' love with their fellow prisoners. Many women became Christians in that terrible place because of the witness of the two sisters. Betsie, 59, died in Ravensbruck. Corrie survived and returned home from the death camp, realizing that her life was a gift from God. At 53, she began a worldwide ministry, sharing what she and Betsie had learned in Ravensbruck. "There is no pit so deep that God's love is not deeper still," and "God will give us the love to be able to forgive our enemies," she would say.

Then years later during a meeting in Germany, she was tested. While she was teaching, she saw a familiar face in the crowd. The face she saw was that of a former guard in one of the camps that incarcerated her. Feelings of bitterness and memories of the death camp welled up inside her. She was teaching about the love of God, its depth and magnitude that was able to overcome any obstacle and no one was aware of the conflict rising inside her. At the altar call, the former guard came forward and said, "Thank you so much for teaching of God's love and how He can forgive anything. It is so wonderful! I can't believe He's forgiven me for what I've done..." and he put out his hand to her. As the man stood with his hand outstretched, a mighty conversation took place between Corrie and her Savior.

*"God, what shall I do?"* Corrie prayed inwardly.

*"Take his hand."* God whispered to her heart.

*"I can't do that..."* she prayed.

*"You're right, you cannot but the love of God that is shed abroad in your heart can."*

*"But I'm angry..."* she whispered.

*"That's right, and you will stay that way until you do what I say,"* God instructed her heart.

Corrie decided to obey and reached forth her hand. She felt nothing, but God manifested Himself in that service in a supernatural way.

Once God forgives, He remembers our sins no more. If we have sinned and asked God for forgiveness and He has given it yet we refuse to forgive ourselves, we make ourselves greater than God. If we refuse to release ourselves from past failures, we are preventing any forward movement and God's blessings. We have thrown ourselves into a pit and, consequently, cannot become what God has created us to be. That is why the Apostle Paul cried out, "Oh wretched man that I am, who shall deliver me from this body of death."

Forgiving and forgetting work in parallel to move us forward to our destiny. If we heed both, we keep the way clear for success. If we live long enough, we are going to fail. Failing is not the worst thing that can happen, quitting is. That is why, no matter how talented or gifted, we must have persistence, that pressing "forward toward the mark for the prize of the high calling of God in Christ Jesus." [256]

## Principle 8. Faithfulness

God commits to faithful men, those who care about the details and who quietly and persistently move forward. "He that is faithful in that which is least is faithful also in much: and he that is unjust in the least is unjust also in much. If therefore ye have not been faithful in the unrighteous mammon, who will commit to your trust the true riches? And if ye have not been faithful in that which is another man's, who shall give you that which is your own?" [257] God owns everything, but He has commissioned us to be co-rulers, co-managers with Him. He will give us all we prove we can handle, and hold us accountable for what He has given us. That is because He expects increase on His investment. To be accounted faithful by God, we must prove ourselves in four areas: (1) in small things; (2) in the management of our personal finances; (3) in the management of another's property; and (4) in the stewardship of God's property.

If we cannot handle small things or pay attention to details, we cannot expect to handle larger tasks. We must become proficient in the small, insignificant things, such as entry-level tasks; otherwise, we will never qualify for a supervisory position. Unless we are faithful at the supervisory level, we cannot expect to be promoted to the managerial level. Therefore, it is important that every day we fulfill the requirements of our current level, striving for excellence with each task.

If we cannot manage our personal finances, how can we expect another to trust us with his? Dreaming of making $400,000 a year will not make it so, especially if we cannot manage $40,000 a year or, worse, $14,000 a year. Personal money management principles apply no matter the amount of the income. If we faithfully apply the principles, we will be surprised how quickly our level of income will change.

We must prove ourselves faithful with that which belongs to another in order to qualify to manage our own business. For example, if we want to own our own business someday, then we should perform our tasks as though we already owned the business and are paying the bills. This is not to say we should develop an attitude of opposing the employer or being difficult to work with; rather, we should observe the rules and perform the tasks as we would want an employee of our business to do.

Finally, we must prove ourselves in the stewardship of God's property.

We do not own what we possess; we are merely stewards. Therefore, we are accountable to God for the care and use of those items. Jesus said, "He who would be greatest in the kingdom of God, let him be the servant of all." This means we are only qualified to lead to the degree that we are willing to serve others.

Because God commits to faithful men, He constantly watches to see which of us qualifies. Paul told Timothy to "commit … to faithful men who will be able to teach others." [258] In other words, the attribute of faithfulness precedes opportunity. When we are faithful, opportunities will come our way, opportunities to reveal the nature of our character. We do not need to pray for opportunities; they will come. We must pray to be ready for them. When we manifest the diligence, discipline and commitment of being a faithful person, then the ability to perform the task will come upon us; we will be ready for the opportunity. Faithfulness, not ability and talent, is the most important element that leads to our God-ordained destiny; faithfulness is. The eyes of the Lord go "to and fro throughout the whole earth to show Himself strong on behalf of those whose hearts" are perfect toward Him. [259] God is looking for faithful men and women, people He can trust with His property, people who are faithful. The reward of the trustworthy is more trust. That person does not need to be the most talented or the most experienced, just the most faithful. All the promises of God and all the favor of God rests upon the faithful person.

The Scriptures tell us that when we are faithful, we will prosper and be promoted. This proving of our character qualifies us.

A faithful man will abound with blessings.

—Proverbs 28:20, NKJV

Moreover it is required in stewards that one be found faithful.

—1 Corinthians 4:2, NKJV

The blessing of the Lord makes one rich, and He adds no sorrow with it.

—Proverbs 10:22 , NKJV

The Lord makes poor and makes rich; He brings low and lifts up.

—1 Samuel 2:7, NKJV

## Principle 9. Never Murmur

This principle could easily be named the law of persistent prayer and praise. If we are perpetually praising God, there is no time for murmuring. Also, since God inhabits the praise of His people, He is ever-present when we are worshipping Him. It is His will that we praise Him; that is why we are instructed to give thanks in everything. [260] Knowing God's will is in doing God's will. In other words, proof of knowing is in the doing. By acting on what God asks us to do, we gain greater revelation of His will and way. One of the instructions from 1 Thessalonians 5, is that we should rejoice evermore. This rejoicing is not because we are *in* certain circumstances, but because we are *going through*. There is a way out, a way to get to the other side. We can rejoice because we do not have to stay in whatever circumstances we find ourselves. God despises murmuring. Just as murmuring kept the children of Israel from entering the Promised Land, so murmuring will keep us from reaching our God-ordained destiny.

Another instruction is that we should delight ourselves in the Lord so that He can give us the desires of our hearts. [261] "Delight" derives from a primitive Greek root, `anag (pronounced aw-nag') meaning "to be soft or pliable." When we delight ourselves in the Lord, we become totally submissive to His will, His Word, and His way. We make ourselves malleable and pliable so that He can shape us and form us and use us to perform His perfect will. This delight can turn to being thankful for our being, our talents, our special gifts, the family heritage, and so forth. But consider for a moment our jobs; how many of us complain about our current jobs and all the time ask God for different ones? Why would God be obligated to answer that prayer? We are to thank God for our present job. We are to thank Him for who we are, for what we are, and for where we are. We are to persist in praise and prayer. When we sing our prayers to the Lord, as King David did, we enter into a realm of praise that allows God's power to be manifested in our lives. God plants His desires in our hearts and when we submit to His desires through praise and submission, He then causes His desires to become our desires, and thus gives us the desires of our heart. His will becomes our will. His way becomes our way. His wisdom becomes our wisdom. He empowers us to live on a different level of understanding and experience. "Do not grow weary in well doing" is another commandment. [262] If we continue to praise and practice the presence of God, we will reap a spiritual harvest that far exceeds any material blessing. This well doing can also extend to acts of charity, which, again, bring their own fulfillment.

Then there is the sacrifice of praise, which is recommended to be continual. "By him therefore let us offer the sacrifice of praise to God continually, that is, the fruit of our lips giving thanks to his name." [263] "The fruit of our lips" is covered by an interesting term, *homologeo,* usually translated "confess" in English; this term, in this setting, means "to confess by celebrating with praise." We have been taught a lot about confession, and we have learned that the words we speak affect our lives and the lives of those around us. But in studying Hebrews 13:15, we learn that God clearly states that confession is to be borne out of a thankful heart. It is a common error for us to be unthankful and confess a lot of things, but God is making it very clear that if we are going to confess and expect it to have a positive effect on our lives that we must confess from a spirit of thanksgiving. Thanksgiving is praising God for what He does; adoration is praising God for who He is. I think Paul aptly named this confession "the sacrifice of praise." It is not easy to confess by celebrating with praise; it becomes a test of our fellowship with God. Only those who genuinely walk close to God have any proficiency at all in this kind of celebration, yet it is open to each of us.

The Scriptures teach us that "the steps of a good man are ordered by the Lord." [264] God does not expect each of us to be at the same level in our spiritual growth. He is content to allow us to grow at our own rate. He places encouragement along our path and offers guidance to enable us to mature in Him. He also says that "a righteous man may fall seven times and rise again" and "though he fall, he shall not be utterly cast down: for the Lord upholdeth him with his hand." [265] Perhaps this is because God wants us to observe the law of persistent prayer and praise.

Jesus came that we might have more abundant life. He rewards us when we diligently seek Him, and part of that reward is the presence and power of the Holy Spirit. As we walk obediently with Him, the more He will entrust us to do. But we will never reach our full potential until we follow God's plan explicitly. However, we will realize His destiny for us incrementally as we walk in His path of obedience. If necessary, God will split the Red Sea, move the sundial back, or cause the sun to stand still to fulfill His plan and purpose for us, especially if we actively honor Him.

## Summary

- God wants to bless us, promote us and reward us.

- God has blessed us, chosen us, and predestined us.

- We are chosen, royal, holy and special. We are God's own possession, purchased by Him.

- We are created by God for a specific purpose. We are special, a work of art.

- God created us for excellence, and for the work of our hands to be productive.

- All true happiness and success are born out of a Christ-like character.

- God has given us *principles* to live by, *promises* to believe in, *examples* to follow, and *commandments* to obey.

- To reach God's ordained destiny, we must go from relationship with God to fellowship with God.

- It pleases God to give us the kingdom.

- Diligence in every area of life brings rewards.

- Meditation is the birthplace of creativity.

- God's anointing of His Spirit in our life will promote us and give us power.

- We must forget the disappointments and the failures of the past before we can embrace the future.

- Faithfulness is the foundation of our character.

- Persistence is prayer, and prayer is the antidote for murmuring. Murmuring will stop the blessings of God in our life.

- Our money represents our life. What we do with it and how we spend it show what is important to us in life.

- If we do not put much of our money into the ministry of God, then we do not have much of our life in the kingdom of God. We will put our money where our heart abides.

- Christlike character is your destiny.

# CHAPTER TEN

## PICKING UP BONUSES THROUGH HONORING GOD

Honoring God is the standard of holiness. When all of our thoughts, words and deeds are to honor God, we will live a holy life. Likewise, the love of truth is the standard of spirituality. Some people love only the truth they want to believe; they are partial. God is neither partial nor incomplete, doubleminded nor unstable. His Word is truth and it teaches that we can know His will. After we have done His will, we can receive the promise of God through faith, patience and endurance. "Therefore do not cast away your confidence, which has great reward. For you have need of endurance, so that after you have done the will of God, you may receive the promise: 'For yet a little while, and He who is coming will come and will not tarry. Now the just shall live by faith; but if anyone draws back, my soul has no pleasure in him.' But we are not of those who draw back to perdition, but of those who believe to the saving of the soul." [266]

Doing the will of God is likened unto running a race with a set course. This course is symbolic of God's plan for our lives. "Therefore we also, since we are surrounded by so great a cloud of witnesses, let us lay aside every weight, and the sin which so easily ensnares us, and let us run with endurance the race that is set before us, looking unto Jesus, the author and finisher of our faith, who for the joy that was set before Him endured the cross, despising the shame, and has sat down at the right hand of the throne of God. For consider Him who endured such hostility from sinners against Himself, lest you become weary and discouraged in your souls." [267]

If we do His will with patience, we will inherit the promises. "And we desire that each one of you show the same diligence to the full assurance of hope until the end, that you do not become sluggish, but imitate those who through faith and patience inherit the promises." [268] The kingdom of God does not operate on charity. It operates on a covenant exchange where the people of God give Him first place in their lives, recognizing Him as their source. If the people break the covenant, then God deals with them justly. There is a story in the book of 1 Samuel about a godly priest named Eli. He knew that his sons were breaking the laws of God, but he did nothing about it except for a mild reprimand. God's judgment included Eli along with his sons: "Therefore, I, the Lord God of Israel, declare that although I promised that your branch of the tribe of Levi could always be my priests, it is ridiculous to think that what you are doing can continue. I will honor only those who honor me, and I will despise those who despise me." [269] It has always been like this: God honors only those who honor Him. Here are four areas in which we can honor God more.

## With our substance

Generally, substance refers to our wealth or money. Money is gained in exchange for our time, talent, education, skills, and so forth. Since all of these things comprise our life, it stands to reason that money represents our life. God has commanded, "Honour the Lord with thy substance, and with the firstfruits of all thine increase." [271] In return, He promises that "thy barns be filled with plenty, and thy presses shall burst out." [271] When we worship at the offering plate, we are returning to God a portion of our life.

Jesus said that our hearts would be where our treasure is. That is why a look at our checkbooks will reveal where our hearts are; where do we spend our money? On golf, fishing, sports, hobbies, pornography? If our hearts are in the kingdom of God, we will put our money there. Our use of money is a visible expression of our faith. What we do with our money represents what we do with our life. What you do with your money, how you spend your money shows what you do with your life. People who do not have much of their life in the kingdom of God, do not put much of their money into the work of God. We can determine the depth of our love for God by the degree that we give to Him. Tithing is an obedient expression of faith that God is our source.

## With obedience

Obedience is better than sacrifice. Jesus said that obedience is the proof of love. Love and passion are not synonymous. Anyone can have a passion for God, but only those who truly love are obedient. We cannot offset by sacrifice what we lose through disobedience. No sacrifice is enough: not prayer, praise, time in fellowship with God, acts of kindness; nothing reaches God's heart like obedience. Prayer will not compensate for the disobedience of not tithing. Malachi tells us that when we tithe God will rebuke the devourer. The enemy devours our finances when we disobey God by not tithing. We cannot sow prayer and reap money, because a harvest is always related to what is sown. Many people pray about their finances, but they are sowing prayer and trying to reap money. We will reap what we sow. We cannot sow apple seeds and reap oranges. We are where we are in every area of our lives because of the seeds we have sown in the past. This is true financially, spiritually, relationally, physically, and intellectually.

Paul wrote in Galatians, "Be not deceived; God is not mocked: for whatsoever a man soweth, that shall he also reap." [272] We must plant for the future rather than just reaping from the past. Every time we plant, whether good or evil, we are saying, "I refuse to stop planting for the future." Our lives are a result of what we have planted. When we sow faithfully into the kingdom with our finances, God is faithful to bring in the harvest. This way we have some control over our destiny. We sow in the present for a future harvest. Since we can only reap from the past, we are reaping today the harvest of the seeds sown in the past. If we do not like the quantity of our harvest, then we increase the amount of the seed we sow in the present. The meaning of our lives is to help as many other people as we can to become what God wants them to be. We are never more like God than when we do that. Even Jesus learned obedience. "Though he were a Son, yet learned he obedience by the things which he suffered; and being made perfect, he became the author of eternal salvation unto all them that obey him." [273] He laid aside His life to help us become what God wants us to be.

## By honoring your wife

The Bible teaches that when a man does not treat his wife right, his prayers will be hindered. "Likewise, ye husbands, dwell with them according to knowledge, giving honour unto the wife, as unto the weaker vessel, and as being heirs together of the grace of life; that your prayers be not hindered." [274] So part of honoring God is honoring one's wife. Ephesians 5:28 teaches that a man should treat his wife the way he would treat himself. If he loves himself, he will love her and treat her as a joint heir. If he does not love himself, then he will become abusive and autocratic. Men who abuse women have an identity problem in their own lives. When the identity problem is addressed and resolved, then the man has a chance to honor his wife. Woman was created to be the helpmeet, the completion, of the man. God saw that man was not complete by himself; there was no ability for procreation, so God created the woman *for* the man. This does not mean that at marriage she becomes his slave, his property. A man does not own his wife; he becomes only the steward of her love. Her love is always a gift; he cannot earn it. If the man is not a proper steward of her, he will ruin their marriage. He cannot treat her however he desires; he cannot force here to be his mate, or his slave. His responsibility is to treat him as he treats himself.

A woman's uniqueness is basically satisfied in relationship to the man. Her fulfillment comes through the reproductive process; in the Old Testament if a woman was barren, she considered it as a curse. That does not mean that she cannot be erudite, an intellectual, an achiever, a careerist, successful or any of these things. She certainly can be. Her uniqueness is what allows her to submit to a man. A man has to minister to her to satisfy that uniqueness in order for her to feel vulnerable so she will be willing to submit; we call that courtship. Courtship is not something that is just between a man and a woman: pastors court their parishioners; corporations court future employees; politicians court the voters. Once the courtship is ended and the marriage solidified, men usually begin to take things for granted and that is the problem. He forgets to continue the courtship and she loses that feeling of vulnerability and uniqueness, so she stops submitting.

Furthermore, Dr. Edwin Louis Cole teaches, "Jesus said a man should love his wife as Christ loves the Church; He was willing to make a total sacrifice to demonstrate His love. Then He demonstrates the qualities of consistency, decisiveness and strength. A wife wants these same qualities from her husband. He must show her his moral strength by restraint and gentleness. A man honors God when he loves his wife as Christ loved the Church."

## By honoring your parents

One of the most interesting Scriptures in the Bible is about giving to parents. Jesus told some of the religious people of His day that they were neglecting their parents in the name of giving to God. Those who made this gift, called *Corban*, would make a rash vow to God that would leave their parents in need. The priests would uphold these gifts because they had been vowed to God and all gifts to God had to be honored, they said. Jesus condemned this practice. "And he said unto them, Full well ye reject the commandment of God, that ye may keep your own tradition. For Moses said, Honour thy father and thy mother; and, Whoso curseth father or mother, let him die the death: but ye say, If a man shall say to his father or mother, It is Corban, that is to say, a gift, by whatsoever thou mightest be profited by me; he shall be free. And ye suffer him no more to do ought for his father or his mother; making the word of God of none effect through your tradition, which ye have delivered: and many such like things do ye." [275]

I actually like the paraphrase of those verses in *The Living Bible* best: "For instance, Moses gave you this law from God: 'Honor your father and mother.' And he said that anyone who speaks against his father and mother must die. But you say it is perfectly all right for a man to disregard his needy parents, telling them, 'Sorry, I can't help you! For I have given to God what I could have given to you.' And so you break the law of God in order to protect your man-made tradition. And this in only one example. There are many, many others." Jesus said that we honor God when we honor our parents.

I found this scripture one evening while reading devotionally before retiring. I had never heard such a doctrine taught from the pulpit. I had tithed faithfully for years, and had often given in offerings and even supported some orphans from time to time; however, when I read this scripture, I was immediately convicted in my heart. My elderly parents, who lived in another state, were disabled, retired, and struggling financially. My mother-in-law, a widow, who lived in another distant part of the country, was subsisting on less than $400 a month. Realizing that God placed such a high priority on the honoring of parents, I suddenly understood that an occasional phone call and greeting card on Mother's Day was not what God had in mind when He commanded us to honor our father and our mother.

Paul repeated this commandment in Ephesians 6:2-3, "Honor your father and mother," which is the first commandment with promise: "that it may be well with you and you may live long on the earth."

Honoring our parents financially is not a request, nor an invitation, nor even a good idea. It is a commandment from God. It is the condition preceding a promise from God. Every promise from a condition attached to it. Here is the promise attached to it: we will live a long, good life and you will prosper. The condition is that we honor our parents. The example of how to honor our parents given by our Lord is to help them financially. When we do what God wants us to do, what will God then do for us? He will bless us and prosper us so we can continue to do the works of God. Honoring our parents is the first commandment with a promise attached to it. Honor your parents and witness the power of God in your life. God delights in our obedience and He will empower us to do progressively more of His will.

These are only four of the ways that we can honor God. He says that He honors those who honor Him. All of us seek His benefits and blessings, often without regard to what we can do for Him. Yet honor carries with it a sense of preciousness, price or costliness, sum as in very expensive, and something of great value, If, indeed, God has become of great value to us so that we cannot endure being without His presence, then honoring Him should be second nature to us. It should be our dearest desire to shower honor upon Him through all of our relationships.

This whole book has been about going beyond the map to establish a relationship with God and to be the kings and priests we have been anointed to be. Any success and any wealth we may attain is based entirely upon that relationship. All our methods, schemes, and plans will come to nought without vital fellowship with Him.

## Summary

- After we have done the will of God, we must have endurance before we will receive the promise.

- We have a covenant with God. When we keep our part of the covenant, God will surely keep His part of the covenant.

- God will honor only those who honor Him.

- We honor God when we give financially to His work.

- We reap in the present from the seeds sown in the past. We sow today for a future harvest. Sow in abundance today for an abundant future harvest.

- Men must honor their wives as joint heirs or their prayers will not be answered.

- Honoring our parents means to help them financially.

# · CHAPTER ELEVEN ·

## MONEY: AN ISSUE OF THE HEART

All of life follows the pattern of relationship, stewardship, and leadership. Our relationship with God and our understanding of the responsibilities inherent in being a child of God will ultimately lead to our influencing others regarding the kingdom of God. This influence is the essence of leadership.

As children of God, we are heirs and joint heirs with Christ in the kingdom. As His children, we also have stewardship responsibilities based on our authority as believers. It is our responsibility to manage the resources of the earth in such a way that the Spirit of God influences every area of life. In other words, we are to have dominion, influence and authority in every area of life.

There can be no dominion without economic dominion. The word "economics" derives from the Greek *oikonomia,* which means "household manager"; *oikonomia* breaks down to its roots: *oikos* (house) plus *nemein* (to manage). All of God's created order is the "house" over which God wants us to exercise faithful stewardship. Economics may not seem important, but it is very important to God. Economics involves the management of material resources, and money is probably the most important material resource in the kingdom of God. In fact, Ecclesiastes says that money is the answer to everything: "A feast is made for laughter, and wine makes merry; but money answers everything" (Ecclesiastes 10:19, NKJV).

Proper stewardship of material resources, i.e., money, establishes influence and authority. Wisdom, Proverbs rightfully tells us, is the principal thing; however, when wisdom is combined with material resources then dominion in all areas of the kingdom is assured. The kingdom of God has always operated on financial resources and it always will. Wisdom is more important than riches, but without the power and influence of money much wisdom is lost to the world. Consider the parable of the wise man who saved a city, but because he was poor his influence was only temporary.

"There was a little city with few men in it; and a great king came against it, besieged it, and built great snares around it. Now there was found in it a poor wise man, and he by his wisdom delivered the city. Yet no one remembered that same poor man. Then I said: 'Wisdom is better than strength. Nevertheless the poor man's wisdom is despised, and his words are not heard'" (Ecclesiastes 9:14–16, NKJV).

If no one is influenced, there is no leadership. Faithful stewardship of all our resources will increase our influence with believers and unbelievers in the kingdom. In some areas of the kingdom, only economic power has influence. When it is necessary to impact the civil government, the commercial government and economic institutions then financial resources coupled with the wisdom and favor of God create a formidable force for the cause of the kingdom.

Therefore, what we know and believe about money is important. Unfortunately, money is the most misunderstood topic in the Bible, even though fully 25 percent of the New Testament addresses economic issues: 200 scriptures deal with salvation and more than 2,000 deal with economics and stewardship. This misunderstanding always destroys opportunity because the image we have regarding money determines how we feel about it. Too few of us understand that money is amoral and that we give money morality or immorality by how we use it.

My first memory of money was my dad giving me a big fifty-cent piece to put into the offering plate at church. I did not know then that money is important to God; putting some in the plate was just part of our tradition. Ours was a legalistic but very religious home where we were never really taught about money. I was the oldest of seven children and we were always tight financially, as you usually are in a big family. We never had a lot of money to take vacations or do other things; everything we did was oriented around our family. But one thing I did learn from my parents was to manage debt. If you manage debt, everything else will take care of itself. The only debts I had as an adult were house and car payments. I didn't use credit cards. If I couldn't afford to pay for something, we simply did not buy it. When I first got married that wasn't true; for about a year I had a credit card. I ran up a $500 balance and paid it off when I got my tax return back; I vowed I would never do that again and I never did. Managing debt is a discipline, and I worked hard to master it. Only later did I learn that money is important to God because it is a gift.

Everything we have in life is a gift from God, and He holds us accountable for what He gives us. As mentioned in an earlier chapter, everything that God does is according to a pattern and based on a principle of His kingdom. Because God gives us principles to live by, promises to believe in, examples to follow and commandments to obey, God tells us everything in His Word that we need to live in financial freedom. Everything.

## What we believe about money is important

The principle that applies to money is the pattern of seedtime and harvest as outlined in Genesis 8:22: planting precedes the harvest. Knowledge is the acquiring of facts, understanding is the interpretation of facts, and wisdom is the application of facts. We can know something but if we don't act on it, it won't do us any good. Hosea 4:6 says, "My people are destroyed for a lack of knowledge." What we believe about money will attract or repel it. Some of us grew up thinking that money is the root of all evil. Yet the Bible says the *love* of money is the root of all evil. Others of us were taught that Jesus said, "You can't worship God and Mammon." That's right, we cannot serve God and serve Mammon, but neither can we serve God and any other idol. In this situation, Jesus was talking about idolatry more than He was talking about money.

Mammon was a Philistine god, who was the spirit of materialism. If we think that money is the solution to our problems, then we are guilty of idolatry and we are serving Mammon, the spirit of materialism—riches and money. The difficulty is not with the money but with the idolatry. The problem with the alcoholic is not alcohol; it is idolatry. Because the alcoholic becomes inebriated, loses his sensibilities so that he can forget his problems, he sees alcohol as the solution to his problems. Since it's a solution to his problems, alcohol is his idol, the focus of his life. The same is true with drug addiction or anything else that we view as a solution to our problems.

Most people think, "If only I had a million dollars, I wouldn't have any problems!" Wrong! A million dollars create more problems than they solve. One of these days you may find out, because God is no respecter of persons; He doesn't play favorites. The Bible says, "the blessing of the Lord maketh rich and He addeth no sorrow to it." What does that mean? There are people that are rich, but they're not happy. There are people that have money but they don't have joy because they have sorrow in trying to manage the money, trying to hang on to it, because it's the center and the focus of their lives. God wants us to have money and He won't add any sorrow with it, if we do not view it as the solution to the problems in our lives.

So long as we view God as our problem-solver, He will give us as much money as we can handle. God's top priority is not our lifestyles; His top priority is the kingdom. God told Abraham: "I will bless you, I will make you a blessing." Abraham is the father of faith and, according to Galatians 3, our spiritual father. If Abraham was to be a blessing to others, he had to be a man of abundance—wouldn't you say that's true? How can we be a blessing unless we have an abundant life? We can't. Yet, we are to be like Abraham, a blessing and a power in the community.

Ecclesiastes says that money is the answer to everything. Faith moves heaven, but money moves earth. So in the kingdom of God, we have God, and we have Christ, and we have five spheres of government. We have the government of our family, *family government;* we have the government of ourselves, *self-government* (God's highest and best for each of us is self-government); we have corporate or *economic government;* then we have *civil government;* and the fifth form of government is *Church government.* Now we are to be conduits, pipelines, of God's blessings to the world. God wants to impact the Church through His Son, and He wants the Church to be like the *ekklesia* of old, and impact every area of government.

## The Church, as the *Ekklesia*

The *ekklesia* in the Hellenic culture was a group of citizens that ruled in civic affairs; they were duly constituted authorities that set the moral tone for their communities. So when Jesus called the Church the "*Ekklesia,*" Rome shuddered in their sandals because they knew what the *ekklesia* really was. The *ekklesia* was not some weak, persecuted minority, it had real power in the communities, and that's what God wants for the Church and for us. But the only way that this is going to happen is through the laity, the ordinary Christian like you and me. First, we have to understand that God wants to give us the kingdom. Luke 12:32 says, "It's the Father's good pleasure to give you the kingdom." Second, although God wants to give us the kingdom, He will not do it through the clergy alone, because there are places in the kingdom that the pastor can't reach. While the pastor has a pulpit in the church, our pulpit is our desk, our car, our computer, our cash register, our garage—whatever it may be, whatever our work is, that is our pulpit and that's where we manifest God's glory.

Isaiah 43:7 says that we were created for God's glory. The glory of God was the presence of God, and the essence of God, and the power of God; and the glory of God was the splendor of God, and the majesty of God, and the honor of God, and the virtue of God, and the dignity of God. That is God's glory. He wants to manifest Himself through us to the world, so that we can be a blessing to others. God wants to bless us, prosper us, promote us and set us on high above all nations of the earth.

God wants us to prosper. Third John 2 says, "I wish above all things that you might prosper and be in good health, even as your soul prospers." Psalm 1:1–3 tells us very clearly that if we meditate on the Word of God day and night, we will be like a tree planted by the rivers of water, that bears fruit in season and whose leaf shall not wither, and whatsoever we do shall prosper! Joshua 1:8 says, if we meditate in this word and observe to do these things, then we will prosper and have good success. Repeatedly, the Bible tells us that God wants us to prosper, as did Abraham, our spiritual father. Abraham could be a blessing to other people because he was blessed. In John 10:10, Jesus says, "I have come that you might have life and have it more abundantly." *Perissos,* the Greek word used for abundantly, means "super-abundance." This means excessive, overflowing surplus, more than enough for us and for other people, because God wants to establish His covenant in you. It is God Who gives us the power—Deuteronomy 8:18—to get wealth so that we might establish His covenant in the earth. If we are pipelines of His blessing to the kingdom, we are going to be blessed in the process.

The purpose of prosperity is not for us to consume it in our own lusts, but for the sake of the kingdom. "Pure religion, and undefiled before God the Father is to visit the widows and orphans in their afflictions." I know a man that gave $25,000 or $30,000 to help build an orphanage in South

America. That orphanage would not be built if God hadn't put it on somebody's heart to help. Billy Graham would never have an evangelistic crusade if somebody weren't prosperous enough to help him. There wouldn't be any missionaries in the world if somebody weren't supporting them. But in order to support them, we have to have abundance. I know a man who bought a house and lets a widow live in it for nothing. He had to have abundance to do that. Another man has made sixty-six trips to the Philippines and has helped start over 400 churches there; he is a businessman, not a preacher. He has abundance in his life because he is using it for the purposes of the kingdom,

Matthew 6:33 says, "Seek ye first the kingdom of God and His righteousness, and all these things shall be added unto you." *These things* are the material things mentioned in the previous verses. The *kingdom of God*, the Amplified Bible says, is "doing things God's way." Seek ye first the kingdom of God, seek ye first *doing things God's way.* God has a way of doing things. Deception comes when we want to do things we think are God's will, but we want to do them our way. That's why we have to know what the Bible says. Because if you've been taught all your life that poverty is a virtue, then you have been taught a lie. The Bible says poverty is a curse. The Bible teaches that if we live a life of obedience, God will prosper us; yet one of the biggest areas of disobedience in our lives is the stewardship of our finances, what we do with our money.

## Pattern of Seedtime and Harvest

We want prosperity, yet we ignore the pattern of seedtime and harvest. Everything God does, He does according to seedtime and harvest. Genesis 8:22 says, "While the earth remains, seedtime and harvest, cold and heat, winter and summer and day and night shall not cease." Is the earth still here? Jesus came by the seed of the woman, and the harvest is His Church. You are the result of seedtime and harvest: there was a nine-month gestation period, and you are the result of it. It's true of the kingdom, spiritually; it's true physically; it's true in agriculture; it's true financially. It's true in every area of our lives—we have to give before we can get. *Givers gain.* Because that is the law of reciprocity.

*Reciprocation* is return in kind or of like value. Luke 6:38 says to give and it shall be given unto you—not to somebody else. Give, and it shall be given unto you, good measure, pressed down, shaken together, running over, shall men give into your bosom. It doesn't say that if you give it's going to fall down from heaven, because that's not the way God does things. He doesn't work through angels or things; God works through other people, mankind. So when you give, men will give back to you. That's the law of reciprocity, which is closely connected to your being created in God's image.

In Genesis 1:26, God said, "Let us make man in our image, according to our likeness, and let them have dominion over everything on the earth." And verse 28 says, "To be fruitful and multiply and fill the earth and subdue it, and have dominion over everything that is on the earth." God created us for dominion. We are created in God's image; we have God's DNA. God says that we are created like Him—God is Love! God so loved the world that He gave His only begotten Son. It is the nature of God to give. If we are created in His image, then it is our nature to give. So if we are not giving, we are not like God—God is love. Love is the characteristic of heaven, and lust is the characteristic of hell. Lust desires to benefit self at the expense of others. If we lust for money so that we can consume it on ourselves, that is a sin. But if we seek money as a means of spreading God's love to other people, God will funnel His blessings through us in a greater way than we ever dreamed or imagined.

Proverbs 3:9–10 says, "Honor the Lord with thy substance and the firstfruits of thine increase, so that your barns may be filled with plenty and your winepresses shall burst forth with new wine." *Substance* means wealth, riches, possessions—your money. Money represents your life, because you go to work every day and exchange your time and your talent and your education for a commodity called money. Your time, your education, your talent, your skills, your work, your efforts, and your focus are your life. So money represents your life, and what you do with your money and how you spend your money shows what you do with your life.

That's why Matthew 6:21 says, "Where your treasure is, there will your heart be also." If you spend money on drugs and alcohol, that's where your heart is. If you spend your money on fishing, that's where your heart is. If you spend your money on golf, like I do, that's where your heart is. You spend your money where your heart is. Money is important to God, because God can see your life by how you spend your money. Do you spend more money on the kingdom of God than you do on your groceries? On your car payment, or your house payment? On anything else? I know a lot of people who do. But they didn't get there overnight, because it's all about seedtime and harvest. Because 20, 30, 40 years ago, they started being faithful with the little things that they had. As time grew, those little things became bigger and bigger and bigger, and those people's affection for God became bigger because they became bigger conduits of blessing to the world.

You are blessed when you do what God wants you to do. He is going to give you more power, more abilities and more resources with which to bless others. If you are supporting missionaries, churches, TV ministries, orphanages and widows around the world, God is going to give you more. It starts right where you are and with the tithe, which is the tenth of everything that you earn every week before taxes are deducted. Why before taxes? Because God wants the firstfruits of your life. God wants to be paid first. If you pay the tithe after taxes are deducted, that means you love the government more than you love God.

Unfortunately, many of us are afraid to put God to the test. But God says, "Prove Me, try Me, test Me" in Malachi 3. Before God promotes you, He will test you. Before God will give you increase in your life, He will test you. Deuteronomy 8:2 says, "I will humble you, to prove you, to know you." He tests you after He humbles you, so you can both humble yourself and come before God, or God will humble you. It's easier to humble yourself than it is for God to humble you. Trust me! He says, "I will humble you to prove you to know you," and then Deuteronomy 8:16 says, "that He might humble you and that He might test you, to do you good in the end"—to see if you will obey His commandments or not.

You can only reap what you sow. Galatians 6 says, "Be not deceived, God is not mocked. As a man soweth, so shall he also reap." Many people with financial difficulties are sowing in prayer and trying to reap money. If you want to get physically stronger, do you pray about it? No! You get some weights and work out. You run, you do whatever it takes. You sow what you want to reap, don't you? You have to give to get. If you want to grow physically stronger, you have to sow exercise. If you want to grow in knowledge, you apply the knowledge you have and sow in study to gain more knowledge. Likewise, if you want to grow financially, you sow money. You can't sow prayer and reap money, it does not work! God says, "To obey is better than sacrifice." If you just obey God, and give into the kingdom of God, you'll reap financial resources; you won't have to pray about it. You won't have to sacrifice prayer to try to reap money. So many people are sacrificing their time, prayer, and tears to try to get money; and it doesn't work. It never has and it never will! You can only reap what you sow.

And you reap in the same measurement that you sowed. II Corinthians 9:6, "But this I say, He who sows sparingly will also reap sparingly, and he who sows bountifully will also reap bountifully. So let each one give as he purposes in his heart, not grudgingly or of necessity, for God loves a cheerful giver. And God is able to make all grace abound toward you, that you, always having all sufficiency in all things, may have an abundance for every good work. As it is written: He has dispersed abroad, he has given to the poor; his righteousness remains forever. Now may he who supplies seed to the sower, and bread for food, supply and multiply the seed you have sown, and increase the fruits of your righteousness, while you are enriched in everything for all liberality, which causes thanksgiving through us to God." In other words, your giving determines the size of the harvest. It's like I told some people in Nicaragua, "If you have a bunch of watermelon seeds and you only throw three or four seeds out, how many watermelons are you going to get next spring? But if you plant tens of thousands of watermelon seeds, you are going to have a bountiful harvest." If you sow into the kingdom of God penuriously, stingily, holding back more than is meet, you're not going to have a big harvest. But if you sow bountifully, liberally, graciously, into the kingdom, then you'll have a big harvest coming back. "God is able to make all grace abound toward you, that you always, having all sufficiency in all things, may abound unto every good work." *Good work* is the operative term. You put your financial resources into good works, then God will bring them back to you so that you can give more.

II Corinthians 9:11 says, "While you are enriched in everything for all liberality." How liberal are you? Do you have a poverty mentality or an abundance mentality? Are you stingy or liberal in the way that you deal with people? When you negotiate a contract, do you try to take all the other person's profit, or do you allow him to have some benefit? When you go out to eat, how large a tip do you leave—10, 15 or 20 percent? Or 25 percent? I never tip less than 20 percent. Never. Sometimes, 25 percent because I want to have a liberal spirit. One of the reasons is, my son was a waiter one year. He used to come home with stories about people who would give him a $2 tip after being at his table for three or four hours. Then he would tell me about the people who would give him a $200 tip.

Are you liberal in your giving into the kingdom of God? When it comes time to write that check and you feel resistance to the amount you want to give, double it! We do this all the time. If I am going to give into a ministry, and I have something that I want to give, and I feel like the enemy is saying, "You cannot afford to do that," or "They don't deserve that, that's too much money," I just go ahead and double it. Because the devil will leave you alone when you start doubling your gift. God wants you to operate out of a liberal, abundant spirit, because that is the Spirit of God.

Look at the liberality and the abundance of nature. I watch the Discovery Channel all the time, and National Geographic. Did you know a fish lays 10,000 eggs! And you, think, "Man! Ten thousand eggs!" But other fish eat them, turtles eat them, birds eat them, but a lot of them live. You see, God deals in abundance. How many seeds are in a watermelon? We believe in zero population growth, right? A man and a woman, two children. God does not operate on zero population growth. God believes in abundance. God is not worried about a population explosion; He is not worried about us using up the resources of this earth.

He is not worried about our using up all the creative ideas. In 1899, the U.S. Patent Office recommended, "You need to close down the Patent Office because all the good ideas have already been discovered." It's true! When it comes to liberality in your spirit, God is going to give you ideas, and thoughts, and visions, and dreams you never had before, because God is spirit and you are spirit. Romans 8:14 says, "Those who live by the Spirit of God, they are the sons of God." When you have a liberal spirit, which is the Spirit of God, manifested in your life, God will give you ideas you never had before.

### Faithfulness Precedes Increase

Proverbs 28:20 says, "A faithful man shall abound with blessings." When I say, "Bless you, Brother!" that means that I am anointing you for increase, and for endowed power to bring prosperity and success in your life. Proverbs 26 says, "But a faithful man, who can find?" Faithful men and women are hard to find. But faithfulness is the cornerstone of your character. Luke 16:10, "He who is faithful in what is least is faithful also in much; and he who is unjust in what is least is unjust also in much."

I worked in a printing company at one time, making $1.30 an hour. This was a long time ago! I worked 12 hours a day, five days a week, from six o'clock in the morning until six o'clock at night. I can remember seeing the owner of the printing company walk in the door wearing a $400 suit. That was a lot of money back then! It would be like a $1,500 suit today.

I remember thinking, "Wow! I wonder what it would be like to own a company like this." If you're not faithful where you are, you will never go beyond where you are. Let's say, for instance, that you are an assembly line worker. If you're not faithful as an assembly line worker, you will never be a line supervisor. When you get promoted to be a line supervisor, if you're not faithful in doing your best and operating in excellence, and being liberal in your spirit, as a line supervisor, you will never be a manager; and you will never be the president; and you will never own the company some day. So unless you're doing your best where you are right now, with all due diligence, you can forget about ever owning your own company, because it will never happen. If you can't tithe on your $10,000 a year, you'll never qualify yourself to make $100,000 a year. Because God will never give it to you. You have to be faithful in the small things as a test to see if you qualify for more responsibility and greater resources. So whatever amount of money it is you are making now, tithe and honor God with what you have.

When my wife and I became Christians, one of the things that really turned my life around was Hebrews 11:6, where it says, "Without faith it is impossible to please Him, for he who comes to God must believe that He is, and that He is a rewarder of those who diligently seek Him." I never knew God wanted to reward me for anything. That wasn't the theology I grew up in. But it's right there in Hebrews: "… He is a rewarder of those who diligently seek him." In response to that scripture, I began to seek God diligently, to read His Word, to understand His Word, to apply His Word to my life; then we started paying tithes and giving offerings. Luke 16:11 says, "Therefore, if you have not been faithful in the unrighteous mammon, who will commit to your trust the true riches?" If you can't live within your budget at $50,000 a year, and you have credit card debt and are paying interest of 18 percent and 20 percent, and you can't manage your resources, you will never make $400,000 or $500,000 a year because God will never allow it. If you can't manage $50,000 a year, how could you ever manage $500,000 a year?

Until you get your current financial house in order, God will not bless you and take you to the next level. You will never have financial freedom until you learn to live without debt. If you can't afford to buy something, then don't buy it! You don't need it! You can live without it! Go in debt for your car and your house, and that's it! As a result, some day you won't owe anything for a car or a house! I haven't made a house payment in I don't know how long! Thank God! But it started 20 years ago when I would not put myself into debt for anything. And it grew.

Get rid of your credit card debt, get out of debt, and you'll start your pathway to financial freedom. It won't happen overnight, because once the seed is planted, it takes time to reap the harvest. As a man sows, so shall he also reap. When you sow into the kingdom of God, you control your destiny because you reap in the present from what you sowed in the past. If you are in debt now, it's because you didn't sow seeds in the past. If you're not prospering, it's not God's fault, it's your fault! If you don't have a harvest coming in, it's because you've never planted the seeds in the past. You plant seeds today for a future harvest; so if you want to have a future harvest, sow liberally today. That gives you some control over your destiny.

If you have not been faithful in what is another man's, who will give you what is your own? To whom does the tithe belong? The tithe is the Lord's! You don't give a tithe to God, you pay it. Because the earth is the Lord's and the fullness thereof, God already owns everything. So when you pay a tithe to God, it's like paying rent. You get to use the building, so you're paying for the right to use it. That's what a tithe is, you're paying God for the right to be here. The tithe is the Lord's, and the offering is yours. You haven't given God anything until you've given an offering. If you refuse to pay the tithe, which already belongs to Him, what have you done? You've robbed from Him! The tithe will rebuke the devourer, but the offering is where the hundredfold return is. My wife and I would give the tithe; then we started giving offerings, whatever we could. Just a little bit, a little here, a little there. But over a period of time our offering equaled our tithe!

Ten years from now, you can have financial freedom. Ten years from now, you can be out of debt. It's possible, if you will sow for the future so that you can reap from the past. Achieving financial freedom is part of the adventure of going beyond the map.

This book has been about going beyond the map in our personal lives or businesses—to places that we have never been before, to see things we have never seen before, and to think thoughts that we have never thought before—all so that we will become what we have never been before.

God wants to take each of us beyond the map to a place He calls Destiny. That is what He wanted for Israel too, but they chose to wander around in the wilderness for forty years, where they were comfortable. They came out of bondage in Egypt, where they had lived in the land of "not enough," and found themselves in the wilderness, the land of "just enough"; but God wanted to take them to the Promised Land, the land of "more than enough." That is where God wants to take each of us as well. It is part of our destiny, and He has a plan for getting us there.

This book has been about doing things God's way, the kingdom way. We have studied the biblical pattern for fulfilling God's ordained destiny, the pattern in which to reach our destination. I hope that you have been challenged by this journey beyond the map, and have discovered the joys, adventures, and fulfillment that have always belonged to you. Reach out and take them for they are yours. They are your destiny.

## Summary

- God has a way of doing things and we should base our lives on His principles.

- God owns the earth and all its fullness.

- Money is important to God because it shows the condition of our hearts and tests our stewardship.

- God wants to establish His kingdom in the earth.

- We have had the wrong perspective about money.

- We have failed to tithe or give offerings.

- We have failed to put the kingdom first.

- God has given us principles to follow.

- The pattern of seedtime and harvest governs life

- It also shows His image, His nature and His way of doing things.

- God's nature is love; love gives.

- God has given us resources to plant into the kingdom.

- He requires of us faithful stewardship.

- He tests our stewardship with the tithe, to see if He can trust us with more.

- It is God's will that we live in abundance.

- He gives us the power and ability to get abundance.

- He teaches us to profit.

- The condition is, we must seek His kingdom first.

- Christlike character is your destiny.

# REFERENCES

## Introduction

1. Ephesians 2:10 For we are His workmanship, created in Christ Jesus for good works, which God prepared beforehand that we should walk in them.

2. 2 Timothy 2:5 And if anyone competes in competitive games, he is not crowned unless he compete lawfully, fairly, according to the rules laid down.

3. Matthew 6:33 TLB But your heavenly Father already knows perfectly well that you need them, and he will give them to you if you give him first place in your life and live as he wants you to.

## Chapter 1. Power of a Dream

4. Proverbs 29:18 KJV. Where there is no vision, the people perish; but he that keepeth the law, happy is he.

5. Jeremiah 29:11-12 TLB. I know the plans I have for you, says the Lord.

6. 1 Corinthians 12:1-31 TLB. I want to write about the special abilities the Holy Spirit gives to each of you.

7. Matthew 25:14-30 NKJV. Story of the talents

8. Ecclesiastes 11:4 TLB. If you wait for perfect conditions, you will never get anything done.

9. Judges 7:14 TLB. Your dream can mean only one thing.

10. 2 Timothy 1:7 NKJV. For God has not given us a spirit of fear, but of power and of love and of a sound mind.

11. Judges 6:12 NKJV. And the Angel of the Lord appeared to him, and said to him, "The Lord is with you, you mighty man of valor!"

12. *Webster's Seventh New Collegiate Dictionary,* (G. & C. Merriam Company, Springfield, MA, 1965), p. 980.

## Chapter 2. It's All About Character

13. Matthew 6:33 NKJV. But seek first the kingdom of God and His righteousness, and all these things shall be added to you.

14. Isaiah 43:7 NKJV. Everyone who is called by My name, whom I have created for My glory; I have formed him, yes, I have made him.

15. Isaiah 43:21 NKJV. This people I have formed for Myself; they shall declare My praise.

16. Hebrews 11:6 NKJV. But without faith it is impossible to please Him, for he who comes to God must believe that He is, and that He is a rewarder of those who diligently seek Him.

17. Psalm 115:12 TLB. Jehovah is constantly thinking about us and he will surely bless us.

18. Isaiah 43:7 TLB. All who claim me as their God will come, for I have made them for my glory; I created them.

19. Ephesians 2:10 KJV. For we are his workmanship, created in Christ Jesus unto good works, which God hath before ordained that we should walk in them.

20. Genesis 1:26 KJV. And God said, Let us make man in our image, after our likeness: and let them have dominion over the fish of the sea, and over the fowl of the air, and over the cattle, and over all the earth, and over every creeping thing that creepeth upon the earth.

21. Romans 8: 16-17 NKJV. The Spirit Himself bears witness with our spirit that we are children of God, and if children, then heirs—heirs

of God and joint heirs with Christ, if indeed we suffer with Him, that we may also be glorfied together.

22.  Matthew 24:43-47 NKJV. "But know this, that if the master of the house had known what hour the thief would come, he would have watched and not allowed his house to be broken into. Therefore you also be ready, for the Son of Man is coming at an hour you do not expect. Who then is a faithful and wise servant, whom his mater made ruler over his household, to give them food in due season? Blessed is that servant whom his master, when he comes, will find so doing. Assuredly, I say to you that he will make him ruler over all his goods."

23.  Genesis 3:15 NKJV. And I will put enmity between you and the woman, and between your seed and her Seed; He shall bruise your head, and you shall bruise His heel.

24.  John 8:32 NKJV. And you shall know the truth, and the truth shall make you free.

25.  2 Corinthians 4:3-4 NKJV. But even if our gospel is veiled, it is veiled to those who are perishing, whose minds the god of this age has blinded, who do not believe, lest the light of the gospel of the glory of Christ, who is the image of God, should shine on them.

26.  2 Corinthians 10:3-5 NKJV. For though we walk in the flesh, we do not war according to the flesh. For the weapons of our warfare are not carnal but mighty in God for pulling down strongholds, casting down arguments and every high thing that exalts itself against the knowledge of God, bringing every thought into captivity to the obedience of Christ.

27.  2 Corinthians 10:3-5 TLB. It is true that I am an ordinary, weak human being, but I don't use human plans and methods to win my battles. I use God's mighty weapons, not those made by men, to knock down the devil's strongholds. These weapons can break down every argument against God and every wall that can be built to keep men from finding him. With these weapons I can capture rebels and bring them back to God and change them into men whose hearts' desire is obedience to Christ.

28. Philippians 4:8 NKJV. Finally, brethren, whatever things are true, whatever things are noble, whatever things are just, whatever things are pure, whatever things are lovely, whatever things are of good report, if there is any virtue and if there is anything praiseworthy— meditate on these things.

29. Romans 12:2 NKJV. And do not be conformed to this world, but be transformed by the renewing of your mind, that you may prove what is that good and acceptable and perfect will of God.

30. Joshua 1:8 NKJV. This Book of the Law shall not depart from your mouth, but you shall meditate in it day and night, that you may observe to do according to all that is written in it. For then you will make your way prosperous, and then you will have good success.

31. Psalm 112:1-10 NKJV. Praise the Lord! Blessed is the man who fears the Lord, who delights greatly in His commandments. His descendants will be mighty on earth; the generation of the upright will be blessed. Wealth and riches will be in his house, and his righteousness endures forever. Unto the upright there arises light in the darkness; he is gracious, and full of compassion, and righteous. A good man deals graciously and lends; he will guide his affairs with discretion. Surely he will never be shaken; the righteous will be in everlasting remembrance. He will not be afraid of evil tidings; his heart is steadfast, trusting in the Lord. His heart is established; he will not be afraid, until he sees his desire upon his enemies. He has dispersed abroad, he has given to the poor; his righteousness endures forever; his horn will be exalted with honor. The wicked will see it and be grieved; he will gnash his teeth and melt away; the desire of the wicked shall perish.

32. Isaiah 54:17 NKJV. No weapon formed against you shall prosper, and every tongue which rises against you in judgment you shall condemn. This is the heritage of the servants of the Lord.

33. Isaiah 48:17 NKJV. Thus says the Lord, your Redeemer, The Holy One of Israel: I am the Lord your God, who teaches you to profit, who leads you by the way you should go.

34. Psalm 5:12 NKJV. For You, O Lord, will bless the righteous; with favor You will surround him as with a shield.

35. Proverbs 4:18 KJV. But the path of the just is as the shining light, that shineth more and more unto the perfect day.

36. Psalm 119:105 NKJV. Your word is a lamp to my feet and a light to my path.

37. Psalm 1:2-3 KJV. In His law he meditates day and night

38. Psalm 1:6 TLB. For the lord watches over all the plans and paths of godly men, but the paths of the godless lead to doom.

39. Isaiah 55:99 NKJV. For as the heavens are higher than the earth, so are My ways higher than your ways, and My thoughts than your thoughts.

40. 2 Timothy 3:16 NKJV. All Scripture is given by inspiration of God, and is profitable for doctrine, for reproof, for correction, for instruction in righteousness.

41. Psalm 103:7 NKJV. He made known His ways to Moses, His acts to the children of Israel.

42. Hosea 4:6 NKJV. My people are destroyed for lack of knowledge. Because you have rejected knowledge, I also will reject you from being priest for Me; because you have forgotten the law of your God, I also will forget your children.

43. Psalm 119: 11, 15-16 NKJV. Your word I have hidden in my heart that I might not sin against You.... I will mediate on Your precepts, and contemplate Your ways. I will delight myself in Your statutes; I will not forget Your word.

44. Psalm 119:148 NKJV. My eyes are awake through the night watches, that I may meditate on Your word.

45. 1 Timothy 4:13-15 NKJV. Till I come, give attention to reading, to exhortation, to doctrine. Do not neglect the gift that is in you, which was given to you by prophecy with the laying on of the hands of the eldership. Meditate on these things; give yourself entirely to them, that your progress may be evident to all.

46. Matthew 12:34 NKJV. For out of the abundance of the heart the mouth speaks.

47. Proverbs 18:20-21 NKJV. A man's stomach shall be satisfied from the fruit of his mouth, from the produce of his lips he shall be filled. Death and life are in the power of the tongue, and those who love it will eat its fruit.

48. Romans 10:8-10 NKJV. But what does it say? "The word is near you, even in your mouth and in your heart" (that is, the word of faith which we preach): that if you confess with your mouth the Lord Jesus and believe in your heart that God has raised Him from the dead, you will be saved. For with the heart one believes unto righteousness, and with the mouth confession is made unto salvation.

49. *Young's Analytical Concordance* (Associated Publishers and Authors, Inc., Grand Rapids, MI, 1972), Index-Lexicon to the New Testament, p. 89.

50. Psalm 35:27-28 NKJV. Let them shout for joy and be glad, who favor my righteous cause; and let them say continually, "Let the Lord be magnified, who has pleasure in the prosperity of His servant." And my tongue shall speak of Your righteousness and of Your praise all the day long.

51. Genesis 8:22 NKJV. "While the earth remains, seedtime and harvest, cold and heat, winter and summer, and day and night shall not cease."

52. Galatians 6:7 NKJV. Do not be deceived, God is not mocked; for whatever a man sows, that he will also reap.

53. 2 Corinthians 9:9:6-7 NKJV. But this I say: He who sow sparingly will also reap sparingly, and he who sows bountifully will also reap bountifully. So let each one give as He purposes in his heart, not grudgingly or of necessity; for God loves a cheerful giver.

54. Luke 16:10-12 TLB.

55. Luke 16:13 TLB.

## Chapter 3. God's Plan for Man

56. 2 Timothy 2:15 KJV. Study to shew thyself approved unto God, a workman that needeth not to be ashamed, rightly dividing the word of truth.

57. 1 Corinthians 10:6, 11 NKJV. Now these things became our examples, to the intent that we should not lust after evil things as they also lusted.... Now all these things happened to them as examples, and they were written for our admonition, on whom the ends of the ages have come.

58. Matthew 25:14-30 NKJV. Parable of the Talents.

59. Matthew 24:14 NKJV.

60. Genesis 2:15 NKJV. Then the Lord God took the man and put him in the garden of Eden to tend and keep it.

61. Genesis 2:19-20 NKJV. Out of the ground the Lord God formed every beast of the field and every bird of the air, and brought them to Adam to see what he would call them. And whatever Adam called each living creature, that was its name. So Adam gave names to all cattle, to the birds of the air, and to every beast of the field. But for Adam there was not found a helper comparable to him.

62. Matthew 25:14 NKJV. For the kingdom of heaven is like a man traveling to a far country, who called his own servants and delivered his goods to them.

63. Matthew 25:14 TLB. Again, the Kingdom of Heaven can be illustrated by the story of a man going into another country, who called together his servants and loaned them money to invest for him while he was gone.

64. Ephesians 3:20 NKJV. Now to Him who is able to do exceedingly abundantly above all that we ask or think, according to the power that works in us.

65. 1 Corinthians 2:9 NKJV. But as it is written: "Eye has not seen, nor ear hears, nor have entered into the heart of man the things which God has prepared for those who love Him."

66. 2 Chronicles 16:9 Young's Literal. His eyes go to and fro in all the earth, to show Himself strong [for] a people whose heart [is] perfect towards Him; thou hast been foolish concerning this, because -- henceforth there are with thee wars.

67. Daniel 11:32 KJV. And such as do wickedly against the covenant shall he corrupt by flatteries: but the people that do know their God shall be strong, and do exploits.

68. Matthew 25:14 NKJV. For the kingdom of heaven is like a man traveling to a far country, who called his own servants and delivered his goods to them.

69. Ephesians 2:10 NKJV. For we are His workmanship, created in Christ Jesus for good works, which God prepared beforehand that we should walk in them.

70. Proverbs 18:16 NKJV. A man's gift makes room for him, and brings him before great men.

71. Matthew 25:14:15 NKJV. And to one he gave five talents, to another two, and to another one, to each according to his own ability; and immediately he went on a journey.

72. Matthew 25:14:15 NKJV. And to one he gave five talents, to another two, and to another one, to each according to his own ability; and immediately he went on a journey.

73. Matthew 25:16-17 NKJV. Then he who had received the five talents went and traded with them, made another five talents. And likewise he who had received two gained two more also.

74. Luke 6:38 NKJV. Give, and it will be given to you: good measure, pressed down, shaken together, and running over will be put into your bosom. For with the same measure that you use, it will be measured back to you.

75. John 3:16 NKJV. For God so loved the world that He gave His only begotten Son, that whosoever believes in Him should not perish but have everlasting life.

76. Matthew 25:18-19 NKJV.

77. Luke 16:10 NKJV. He who is faithful in what is least is faithful also in much; and he who is unjust in what is least is unjust also in much.

78. Luke 16:10-13 NKJV. He who is faithful in what is least is faithful also in much; and he who is unjust in what is least is unjust also in

much. Therefore if you have not been faithful in the unrighteous mammon, who will commit to your trust the true riches? And if you have not been faithful in what is another man's who will give you what is your own?

79.  Romans 2:11 KJV.

80.  Matthew 25:20-22 NKJV. So he who had received five talents came and brought five other talents, saying, 'Lord, you delivered to me five talents; look, I have gained five more talents besides them.' His lord said to him, 'Well done, good and faithful servant; you were faithful over a few things, I will make you ruler over many things. Enter into the joy of your lord.' He also who had received two talents came and said, 'Lord, you delivered to me two talents; look, I have gained two more talents besides them.' His lord said to him, 'Well done, good and faithful servant; you were faithful over a few things, I will make you ruler over many things. Enter into the joy of your lord.'

81.  Matthew 25:23-24 NKJV. His lord said to him, 'Well done, good and faithful servant; you were faithful over a few things, I will make you ruler over many things. Enter into the joy of your lord. Then he who had received the one talent came and said, 'Lord, I knew you to be a hard man, reaping where you have not sown, and gathering where you have not scattered seed.'

82.  Luke 12:48 NKJV. But he who did not know, yet committed things deserving of stripes, shall be beaten with few. For everyone to whom much is given, from him much will be required; and to whom much has been committed, of him they will ask the more.

83.  Matthew 13:12 NKJV. For whoever has, to him more will be given, and he will have abundance; but whoever does not have, even what he has will be taken away from him.

84.  Matthew 25:25 NKJV. 'And I was afraid, and went and hid your talent in the ground. Look, there you have what is yours.'

85.  Proverbs 24:16 NAS. For a righteous man falls seven times, and rises again, But the wicked stumble in time of calamity.

86.  Matthew 25:26-27 NKJV. But his lord answered and said to him,

'You wicked and lazy servant, you knew that I reap where I have not sown, and gather where I have not scattered seed. Therefore you ought to have deposed my money with the bankers, and at my coming I would have received back my own with interest.'

87.  3 John 2 NKJV. Beloved, I pray that you may prosper in all things and be in health, just as your soul prospers.

88.  Psalm 24:1 NKJV. The earth is the Lord's, and all its fullness, the world and those who dwell therein.

89.  Genesis 1:26, 28 NKJV. Then God said, "Let Us make man in Our image, according to Our likeness; let them have dominion over the fish of the sea, over the birds of the air, and over the cattle, over all the earth and over every creeping things that creeps on the earth."… Then God blessed them, and God said to them, "Be fruitful and multiply; fill the earth and subdue it; have dominion over the fish of the sea, over the birds of the air, and over every living thing that moves on the earth."

90.  Ecclesiastes 10:19 NKJV. A feast is made for laughter, and wine makes merry; but money answers everything.

91.  Matthew 25:28-29 NKJV. 'Therefore take the talent from him, and give it to him who has ten talents. For to everyone who has, more will be given, and he will have abundance; but from him who does not have, even what he has will be taken away.

92.  Luke 12:32 NKJV. Do not fear, little flock, for it is your Father's good pleasure to give you the kingdom.

93.  2 Chronicles 16:9 NKJV. For the eyes of the Lord run to and fro throughout the whole earth, to show Himself strong on behalf of those whose heart is loyal to Him. In this you have done foolishly; therefore from now on you shall have wars.

94.  James 4:17 NKJV. Therefore, to him who knows to do good and does not do it, to him it is sin.

95.  Matthew 25:30 NKVJ. And cast the unprofitable servant into the outer darkness. There will be weeping and gnashing of teeth.

96. Proverbs 18:16 NKJV. A man's gift makes room for him, and brings him before great men.

97. John 10:10 NKJV. The thief does not come except to steal, and to kill, and to destroy. I have come that they may have life, and that they may have it more abundantly.

98. 3 John 2 NKJV. Beloved, I pray that you may prosper in all things and be in health, just as your soul prospers.

99. 1 John 2:20 NKJV. But you have an anointing from the Holy One, and you know all things.

100. 1 John 2:27 NKJV. But the anointing which you have received from Him abides in you, and you do not need that anyone teach you; but as the same anointing teaches you concerning all things, and is true, and is not a lie, and just as it has taught you, you will abide in Him.

## Chapter 4. Dominion Commission

101. Isaiah 43:7, NKJV. Everyone who is called by My name, whom I have created for My glory; I have formed him, yes, I have made him.

102. Genesis 1:26-28, NKJV. Then God said, "Let Us make man in Our image, according to Our likeness; let them have dominion over the fish of the sea, over the birds of the air, and over the cattle, over all the earth and over every creeping thing that creeps on the earth." So God created man in His own image; in the image of God He created him; male and female He created them. Then God blessed them, and God said to them, "Be fruitful and multiply; fill the earth and subdue it; have dominion over the fish of the sea, over the birds of the air, and over every living thing that moves on the earth."

103. Matthew 28:17-20, NKJV.

104. Revelation 1:4-6, NKJV.

105. 1 Samuel 10:1. Then Samuel took a vial of oil, and poured it upon his head, and kissed him, and said, Is it not because the Lord hath anointed thee to be captain over his inheritance? 1 Samuel 16:13. Then Samuel took the horn of oil, and anointed him in the midst of

his brethren: and the Spirit of the Lord came upon David from that day forward.

106. 1 Timothy 3:1-6, NKJV. This is a faithful saying: If a man desires the position of a bishop, he desires a good work. A bishop then must be blameless, the husband of one wife, temperate, sober-minded, of good behavior, hospitable able to teach; not given to wine, not violent, not greedy for money, but gentle, not quarrelsome, not covetous; one who rules his own house well, having his children in submission with all reverence (for if a man does not know how to rule his own house, how will he take care of the church of God?); not a novice, lest being puffed up with pride he fall into the same condemnation as the devil.

107. Titus 1:6-9, NKJV. If a man is blameless, the husband of one wife, having faithful children not accused of dissipation or insubordination. For a bishop must be blameless, as a steward of God, not self-willed, not quick-tempered, not given to wine, not violent, not greedy for money, but hospitable, a lover of what is good, sober-minded, just, holy, self-controlled, holding fast the faithful word as he has been taught, that he may be able, by sound doctrine, both to exhort and convict those who contradict.

108. Luke 15:13, NKJV. And not many days after the younger son gathered all together, and took his journey to a far country, and there wasted his substance with riotous living.

109. Biblesoft's *New Exhaustive Strong's Numbers and Concordance with Expanded Greek-Hebrew Dictionary.* (Copyright 1994, Biblesoft and International Bible Translators, Inc.).

110. W. E. Vine, *Vine's Expository Dictionary of Biblical Words,* (Nashville, Thomas Nelson Publishers, 1985).

111. W. E. Vine, *Vine's Expository Dictionary of Biblical Words,* (Nashville, Thomas Nelson Publishers, 1985).

112. Psalm 144:1, NKJV.

113. Proverbs 10:22, NKJV.

114. Genesis 1:28, KJV. And God blessed them, and God said unto them,

Be fruitful, and multiply, and replenish the earth, and subdue it; and have dominion over the fish of the sea, and over the fowl of the air, and over every living thing that moveth upon the earth.

115. W. E. Vine, M.A., *An Expository Dictionary of New Testament Words.* (Lynchburg, Virginia, The Old-Time Gospel Hour), p. 574-575.

116. Psalm 144:1, TLB.

117. Psalm 44:3, NKJV.

118. Psalm 60:12, NKJV.

119. Daniel 11:32, NKJV.

120. Hebrews 6:10-12, NKJV.

121. Galatians 6:9, NKJV.

122. 1 Peter 4:10-11, NKJV.

123. Matthew 6:24, NKJV.

124. Luke 16:10-12, NKJV.

125. Proverbs 22:29, NKJV. Do you see a man who excels in his work? He will stand before kings; he will not stand before unknown men.

126. Ephesians 2:10, NKJV. For we are His workmanship, created in Christ Jesus for good works, which God prepared beforehand that we should walk in them.

127. 1 Peter 4:10-11, NKJV.

128. Isaiah 48:17, NKJV.

129. Deuteronomy 8:18, NKJV.

130. 1 Corinthians 3:8-17, NLTki

## Chapter 5. God Works Through Patterns

131. Matthew 6:33, NKJV. But seek first the kingdom of God and His righteousness, and all these things shall be added to you.

132. 1 Samuel 13:11-15, NKJV.

133. Deuteronomy 20:1-4, NKJV.

134. 2 Samuel 12:1-15, NKJV. Then the Lord sent Nathan to David. And he came to him, and said to him: "There were two men in one city, one rich and the other poor. The rich man had exceedingly many flocks and hers. But the poor man had nothing, except one little ewe lamb which he had bought and nourished; and it grew up together with him and with his children. It ate of his own food and drank from his own cup and lay in his bosom; and it was like a daughter to him. And a traveler came to the rich man, who refused to take from his own flock and from his own herd to prepare one for the wayfaring man who had come to him; but he took the poor man's lamb and prepared it for the man who had come to him." So David's anger was greatly aroused against the man, and he said to Nathan, "As the Lord lives, the man who has done this shall surely die! And he shall restore fourfold for the lamb, because he did this thing and because he had no pity." Then Nathan said to David, "You are the man! Thus says the Lord God of Israel: 'I anointed you king over Israel, and I delivered you from the hand of Saul. I gave you your master's house and your master's wives into your keeping, and gave you the house of Israel and Judah. And if that has been too little, I also would have given you much more! Why have you despised the commandment of the Lord, to do evil in His sight? You have killed Uriah the Hittite with the sword; you have taken his wife to be your wife, and have killed him with the sword of the people of Ammon. Now therefore, the sword shall never depart from your house, because you have despised Me, and have taken the wife of Uriah the Hittite to be your wife.' "Thus says the Lord: 'Behold, I will raise up adversity against you from your own house; and I will take your wives before your eyes and give them to your neighbor, and he shall lie with your wives in the sight of this sun. For you did it secretly, but I will do this thing before all Israel, before the sun.'" So David said to Nathan, "I have sinned against the Lord." And Nathan said to David, "The Lord also has put away your sin; you shall not die. However, because by this deed you have given great occasion to the enemies of the Lord to blaspheme, the child also who is born to you shall surely die." Then Nathan departed to his house.

135. 2 Samuel 11:1, NKJV.

136. Revelation 1:5b-6, NKJV.

137. Proverbs 29:18, TLB. Where there is ignorance of God, the people run wild; but what a wonderful thing it is for a nation to know and keep his laws!

138. Proverbs 29:18, Spanish translation

139. Proverbs 1:32, KJV. For the turning away of the simple shall slay them, and the prosperity of fools shall destroy them.

140. Psalm 53:1, NKJV.

141. James 5:1-4, NKJV.

142. 1 John 2:20, 27, NKJV.

143. Exodus 31:1-6, AMP.

144. 1 John 2:15-16, NKJV. Do not love the world or the things of the world. If anyone loves the world, the love of the Father is not in him. For all that is in the world—the lust of the flesh, the lust of the eyes, and the pride of life—is not of the Father but is of the world.

145. Deuteronomy 17:16, NKJV. But he shall not multiply horses for himself, nor cause the people to return to Egypt to multiply horses, for the Lord has said to you, 'You shall not return that way again.'

146. Ecclesiastes 10:5-7, NKJV. There is an evil I have seen under the sun, as an error proceeding from the ruler: Folly is set in great dignity, while the rich sit in a lowly place. I have seen servants on horses, while princes walk on the ground like servants.

147. Psalm 20:7, NJKV. Some trust in chariots, and some in horses; but we will remember the name of the Lord our God.

148. Psalm 33:17, NJKV. A horse is a vain hope for safety; neither shall it deliver any by its great strength.

149. Leviticus 18:3, NJKV. According to the doings of the land of Egypt, where you dwelt, you shall not do; and according to the doings of

the land of Canaan, where I am bringing you, you shall not do; nor shall you walk in their ordinances.

150. Deuteronomy 17:17, NKJV. Neither shall he multiply wives for himself, lest his heart turn away; nor shall he greatly multiply silver and gold for himself.

151. 1 Kings 11:1-6, NKJV. But King Solomon loved many foreign women, as well as the daughter of Pharaoh: women of the Moabites, Ammonites, Edomites, Sidonians, and Hittites—from the nations of whom the Lord had said to the children of Israel, "You shall not intermarry with them, nor they with you. For surely they will turn away your hearts after their gods." Solomon clung to these in love. And he had seven hundred wives, princesses, and three hundred concubines; and his wives turned away his heart. For it was so, when Solomon was old, that his wives turned his heart after other gods; and his heart was not loyal to the Lord his God, as was the heart of his father David. For Solomon went after Ashtoreth the goddess of the Sidonians, and after Milcom the abomination of the Ammonites. Solomon did evil in the sight of the Lord, and did not fully follow the Lord as did his father David.

152. Deuteronomy 17:17.

153. 1 Kings 12:4, NKJV. Your father made our yoke heavy; now therefore, lighten the burdensome service of your father, and his heavy yoke which he put on us, and we will serve you..

154. Psalm 62:10, NKJV. Do not trust in oppression, nor vainly hope in robbery; if riches increase, do no set your heart on them.

155. 1 Chronicles 29:3-4, NKJV. Moreover, because I have set my affection on the house of my God, I have given to the house of my God, over and above all that I have prepared for the holy house, my own special treasure of gold and silver; three thousand talents of gold, of the gold of Phir, and seven thousand talents of refined silver, to overlay the walls of the houses.

156. Deuteronomy 17:4-20.

157. Hosea 8:12, NKJV. I have written for him the great things of My law, but they were considered a strange thing.

158. Psalm 1:2-3, NKJV. But his delight is in the law of the Lord, and in His law he meditates day and night. He shall be like a tree planted by the rivers of water, that brings forth its fruit in its season, whose leaf also shall not wither, and whatever he does shall prosper.

159. Concepts for developing kingship were taken from *Matthew Henry's Commentary on the Whole Bible*: New Modern Edition, Electronic Database. Copyright 1991 by Hendrickson Publishers, Inc.

## Chapter 6. Getting Wisdom

160. Proverbs 4:7, TLB.

161. Proverbs 16:16, TLB.

162. Proverbs 17:16, TLB.

163. Proverbs 4:8-9, TLB.

164. Proverbs 3:16-18, NJKV. Length of days is in her right hand; and in her left hand riches and honour. Her ways are ways of pleasantness, and all her paths are peace. She is a tree of life to those who take hold of her: and happy are all who retain her.

165. Vine, W. E., *An Expository Dictionary of New Testament Words,* (Lynchburg, VA: Old-Time Gospel Hour), p. 1233.

166. Proverbs 9:10, NKJV.

167. John 1:12-13, KJV. But as many as received him, to them gave he power to become the sons of God, even to them that believe on his name, which were born, not of blood, nor of the will of the flesh, nor of the will of man, but of God.

168. Ephesians 3:9-11, KJV. And to make all men see what is the fellowship of the mystery, which from the beginning of the world hath been hid in God, who created all things by Jesus Christ: to the intent that now unto the principalities and power in heavenly places. According to the eternal purpose which he purposed in Christ Jesus our Lord.

169. James 3:13-18, NKJV.

170. Psalm 111:10, KJV.

171. Proverbs 8:13, KJV.

172. Proverbs 1:29-33, TLB.

173. 1 John 5:4, KJV. For whatsoever is born of God overcometh the world: and this is the victory that overcometh the world, even our faith.

174. Matthew 23:12, KJV. And whosoever shall exalt himself shall be abased; and he that shall humble himself shall be exalted.

175. Luke 1:52, KJV. He hath put down the mighty from their seats and exalted them of low degree.

176. 1 Peter 5:5, KJV. Likewise, ye younger, submit yourselves unto the elder. Yea, all of you be subject one to another, and be clothed with humility: for God resisteth the proud, and giveth grace to the humble.

177. James 4:6, KJV. But he giveth more grace. Wherefore he saith, God resisteth the proud, but giveth grace unto the humble.

178. Ezekiel 28:11, 17, KJV. Moreover the word of the Lord came unto me, saying…Thine heart was lifted up because of thy beauty, thou has corrupted thy wisdom by reason of thy brightness: I will cast thee to the ground, I will lay thee before kings, that they may behold thee.

179. James 1:5, KJV. If any of you lack wisdom, let him ask of God, that giveth to all men liberally, and upbraideth not; and it shall be given him.

180. Matthew 11:29, KJV. Take my yoke upon you, and learn of me; for I am meek and lowly in heart: and ye shall find rest unto your souls.

181. Luke 18:14, KJV. I tell you, this man went down to his house justified rather than the other: for every one that exalteth himself shall be abased; and he that humbleth himself shall be exalted.

182. John 5:19, KJV Then answered Jesus and said unto them, Verily, verily, I say unto you, The Son can do nothing of himself, but what he seeth the Father do: for what things soever he doeth, these also doeth the Son likewise.

183. Luke 22:27, KJV. For whether is greater, he that sitteth at meat, or

he that serveth? Is not he that sitteth at meat? but I am among you as he that serveth?

184. Matthew 8:14, KJV.

185. Matthew 5:3, 5, KJV. Blessed are the poor in spirit: for theirs is the kingdom of heaven.... Blessed are the meek: for they shall inherit the earth.

186. 1 Peter 5:5, KJV. Likewise, ye younger, submit yourselves unto the elder. Yea, all of you be subject one to another, and be clothed with humility: for God resisteth the proud and giveth grace to the humble.

187. Romans 12:10, 15-16, TLB.

188. 1 John 4:20-21, NKJV. If someone says, "I love God," and hates his brother, he is a liar; for he who does not love his brother whom he has seen, how can he love God whom he has not seen? And this commandment we have from Him: that he who loves God must love his brother also.

## Chapter 7. Without Hope, Faith Is Unnecessary

189. Vine, W. E., *An Expository Dictionary of New Testament Words,* (Lynchburg, VA: Old-Time Gospel Hour) p. 562.

190. Titus 1:2, TLB and KJV.

191. 1 Peter 1:20-21, KJV.

192. Colossians 1:27, KJV.

193. 1 Timothy 1:1.

194. Hebrews 11:1

195. Romans 15:13, NKJV

196. Hebrews 11:6, KJV.

## Chapter 8. Kicking the Comfort Zone

197. Hebrews 4:12

198. James 4:17, KJV. Therefore to him that knoweth to do good, and doeth it not, to him it is sin.

199. Proverbs 18:16, KJV.

200. 2 Timothy 3:16-17, NKJV. All Scripture is given by inspiration of God, and is profitable for doctrine, for reproof, for correction, for instruction in righteousness, that the man of God may be complete, thoroughly equipped for every good work.

201. John 16:7, KJV.

202. John 10:10, KJV. The thief cometh not, not for to steal, and to kill, and to destroy: I am come that they might have life, and that they might have it more abundantly.

## Chapter 9. Principles of Career Advancement

203. 1 Peter 2:9, KJV.

204. Psalm 115:12, TLB. Jehovah is constantly thinking about us and he will surely bless us.

205. Hebrews 13:20-21, KJV. Now the God of peace, that brought again from the dead our Lord Jesus, that great shepherd of the sheep, through the blood of the everlasting covenant, make you perfect in every good work to do his will, working in you that which is wellpleasing in his sight through Jesus Christ; to whom be glory for ever and ever. Amen.

206. Jeremiah 29:11, TLB. For I know the plans I have for you, says the Lord. They are plans for good and not for evil, to give you a future and a hope.

207. Ephesians 2:10, NKJV. For we are His workmanship, created in Christ Jesus for good works, which God prepared beforehand that we should walk in them.

208. Ephesians 1:3-5, NKJV. Blessed be the Lord and Father of our Lord

Jesus Christ, who has blessed us with every spiritual blessing in the heavenly places in Christ, just as He chose us in Him before the foundation of the world, that we should be holy and without blame before Him in love, having predestined us to adoption as sons by Jesus Christ to Himself, according to the good pleasure of His will.

209. Proverbs 29:18.

210. 2 Chronicles 16:9, KJV.

211. Ephesians 1:3-5, KJV. Blessed be the God and Father of our Lord Jesus Christ, who hath blessed us with all spiritual blessing in heavenly places in Christ: according as he hath chosen us in him before the foundation of the world, that we should be holy and without blame before him in love: having predestinated us unto the adoption of children by Jesus Christ to himself, according to the good pleasure of his will.

212. 2 Corinthians 9:8, KJV. And God is able to make all grace abound toward you; that ye, always having all sufficiency in all things, may abound to every good work.

213. Philippians 1:6, KJV.

214. Colossians 1:10, KJV. That ye might walk worthy of the Lord unto all pleasing, being fruitful in every good work, and increasing in the knowledge of God.

215. 2 Timothy 2:21, KJV. If a man therefore purge himself from these, he shall be a vessel unto honour, sanctified, and meet for the master's use, and prepared unto every good work.

216. 2 Timothy 3:17, KJV. That the man of God may be perfect, thoroughly furnished unto all good works.

217. Titus 2:14, KJV. Who gave himself for us, that he might redeem us from all iniquity, and purify unto himself a peculiar people, zealous of good works. Titus 3:8, KJV. This is a faithful saying, and these things I will that thou affirm constantly, that they which have believed in God might be careful to maintain good works. These things are good and profitable unto men.

218. 1 Peter 2:12, KJV. Having your conversation honest among the Gentiles: that, whereas they speak against you as evildoers, they may by your good works, which they shall behold, glorify God in the day of visitation.

219. Psalm 37:23, KJV. The steps of a good man are ordered by the Lord: and he delighteth in his way.

220. Daniel 11:32, TLB. He will flatter those who hate the things of God and win them over to his side. But the people who know their God shall be strong and do great things.

221. Psalm 115:12-15, KJV. The Lord hath been mindful of us: he will bless us; he will bless the house of Israel; he will bless the house of Aaron. He will bless them that fear the Lord, both small and great. The Lord shall increase you more and more, you and your children. Ye are blessed of the Lord which made heaven and earth.

222. Isaiah 43:21, KJV. This people have I formed for myself; they shall shew forth my praise.

223. Isaiah 43:7, NKJV. Everyone who is called by My name, whom I have created for My glory; I have formed him, yes, I have made him.

224. Proverbs 8:20-21, KJV. I lead in the way of righteousness, in the midst of the paths of judgment; that I may cause those that love me to inherit substance; and I will fill their treasures.

225. Matthew 6:33, KJV.

226. Hebrews 11:1, NKJV.

227. Hebrews 11:6, NKJV.

228. Acts 3:2-5, KJV (italics added).

229. Psalm 37:4, NKJV.

230. Isaiah 58:14, TLB, (italics added).

231. Luke 12:32, KJV. Fear not, little flock; for it is your Father's good pleasure to give you the kingdom.

232. 2 Chronicles 16:9, KJV. For the eyes of the Lord run to and fro

throughout the whole earth, to shew himself strong in the behalf of them whose heart is perfect toward him. Herein thou hast done foolishly: therefore from henceforth thou shalt have wars.

233. Hebrews 11:5, KJV.

234. Isaiah 30:21, KJV. And thine ears shall hear a word behind thee, saying, This is the way, walk ye in it, when ye turn to the right hand, and when ye turn to the left.

235. Ecclesiastes 9:10, NKJV.

236. Colossians 3:17, KJV.

237. Colossians 3:23, KJV.

238. Proverbs 22:29, KJV.

239. Proverbs 12:24, KJV.

240. Proverbs 13:4, KJV.

241. Proverbs 21:5, KJV.

242. Deuteronomy 11:13-15, KJV, italics added.

243. Psalm 1:1-3, KJV.

244. Joshua 1:8, TLB.

245. Psalm 119:11, NKJV.

246. 1 Timothy 4:13-15, KJV.

247. Deuteronomy 8:18, NKJV (italics added).

248. 1 John 2: 20, 27, KJV.

249. Isaiah 30:21, NKJV.

250. 2 Corinthians 1:21, KJV.

251. Daniel 5:12, NKJV.

252. Isaiah 43:18-19, NIV.

253. Philippians 3:13-14, NKJV (italics added).

254. Proverbs 24:16, NKJV.

255. Mark 11:25, KJV.

256. Philippians 3:14.

257. Luke 16:10-12, KJV.

258. 2 Timothy 2:2, NKJV.

259. 2 Chronicles 16:9, NKJV.

260. 1 Thessalonians 5:16-18, KJV. Rejoice evermore. Pray without ceasing. In every thing give thanks: for this is the will of God in Christ Jesus concerning you.

261. Psalm 37:4-5, KJV. Delight thyself also in the Lord; and he shall give thee the desires of thine heart. Commit thy way unto the Lord; trust also in him; and he shall bring it to pass.

262. Galatians 6:9, KJV. And let us not be weary in well doing: for in due season we shall reap, if we faint not.

263. Hebrews 13:15.

264. Psalm 37:23, NKJV

265. Proverbs 24:16, NKJV, and Psalm 37:24, KJV.

## Chapter 10. Picking Up Bonuses Through Honoring God

266. Hebrews 10:35-39, NKJV.

267. Hebrews 12:1-3, NKJV.

268. Hebrews 6:11-12, NKJV.

269. 1 Samuel 2:30, TLB.

270. Proverbs 3:9 KJV.

271. Proverbs 3:10.

272. Galatians 6:7, KJV.

273. Hebrews 5:8-9 KJV.

274. 1 Peter 3:7 KJV.

275. Mark 7:9-13, KJV.

# IMN
## INTERNATIONAL
## MEN'S NETWORK

Providing the resources to grow the men of
tomorrow, today.

To view all products, events, and materials offered through
International Men's Network, visit us at:

http://www.imnonline.org

**Looking to publish a book
for men?  We can help you!**

If you would like information
about partnering with Guy Thing
Press to publish your message to
the men of the world, visit us
online at:

**www.guythingpress.com**

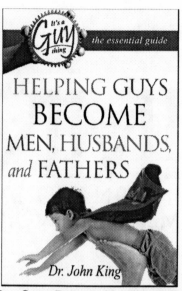

**Helping Guys Become Men, Husbands, and Fathers**
*Dr. John King*

Written for men by a man who believes in the critical and vital role husbands and fathers play in the family, the community, and the world.

Every member of the family needs a man's wisdom, protection, and love to fully develop. Unfortunately, fatherlessness is an epidemic leaving us with "... a generation of boys, raised by women, who don't know what it is to be a man, husband, or father."

You can be a great man, husband, and father...

ISBN: 0-7684-2371-6 | Paperback | 183 Pages

---

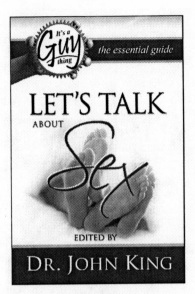

**Let's Talk About Sex**
*Dr. John A. King*

Newspapers today are littered with stories of people falling to sex. Children no longer get a pure view of sex from the Bible, but a distorted image from Hollywood and school.

Let's Talk About Sex delves into the grey area of sex and deals with such topics as:

- How much sex is enough sex?
- Pornography
- What the Bible says about masturbation, oral sex, and sex toys (and everything else you always wanted to ask your pastor, but couldn't.)

ISBN: 0-9786291-3-2 | Paperback

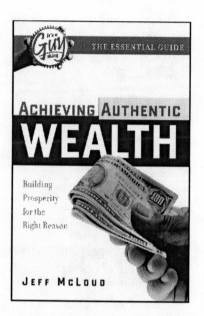

### Achieving Authentic Wealth
*Jeff McLoud*

Wealth and prosperity are not just the multiplication of money. Luke 12:15 says "... a man's life does not consist in the abundance of his possessions." What does it consist of? Some "lay up for *themselves* treasure on earth," while others spend their lives "laying up treasure in heaven."

Jeff McLoud will show you the true meaning of prosperity and how you can achieve it in a way that honors your family, honors your church, and honors your God.

ISBN: 0-9776484-7-8 | Paperback

 **guy thing press** providing the resources for guys who want to be men
visit our website at www.guythingpress.com

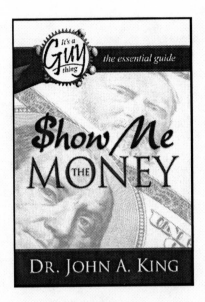

**Show Me the Money**
*Dr. John A. King*

Time Magazine asked, "Does God want you to be rich?" We Say, "No, God wants you to be wealthy." In this book, you will see the fundamentals of creating and using wealth in God's Kingdom.

This book looks at the question of money. Is there such a thing as having too much money? And is money itself the issue? You will find a new revelation of what it means to be wealthy, and God intended for you to be that way.

ISBN: 0-9786291-6-7 | Paperback

**Creating a Better Life**
*Erik Kudlis*

Everyone wants to have a better life, but wanting
that life and having that life are two very different
and oftentimes frustrating things.

In this book by Erik Kudlis, you will learn to
work with God using three simple, yet practical,
keys that every man can establish in his life.

It is possible. You can create a better life.

ISBN: 0-9786291-4-0 | Paperback

 **providing the resources for guys who want to be men**
visit our website at www.guythingpress.com

Printed in the United States
88470LV00005B/79-102/A